THE NECTAR OF SELF-AWARENESS

श्री संत ज्ञानेश्वर

by
Jnaneshwar Maharaj

English Renditions by Swami Abhayananda

ISBN-0-914602-49-7

This book is lovingly offered
At the lotus-feet
Of Baba Muktananda --
By whose grace
All good works are accomplished.

CONTENTS

PREFACE

One of the holy places Baba Muktananda always recommends
that pilgrims visit is the samadhi shrine of Saint Jnaneshwar
at Alandi, about a hundred miles from Baba's ashram in Ganeshpuri.
Baba has great love and reverence for Jnaneshwar and practically
every year pays his respects to him by visiting his shrine with a
large group of devotees. Before he began his third world tour,
Baba sent a beautiful gift of a large silver cover for the alter
stone of the shrine.

Baba often talks about the greatness of Jnaneshwar. He says
that he became convinced of Jnaneshwar's omniscience when he came
across a passage in the Amritanubhava which reads, "Sadashiva, in
the Shiva Sutras, has declared that knowledge is bondage."
Jnaneshwar actually quotes the sutra jnanam bandhah. Now,
Jnaneshwar had not visited far off Kashmir in the north, where
these Shiva Sutras originated, nor had the Shiva Sutras spread to
the south, where he lived. It was not easy to travel long
distances at that time, bullock carts and walking being the only
means of transportation. Then how did Jnaneshwar know about the
Shiva Sutras? He must have known them intuitively.

The Amritanubhava is Jnaneshwar's unique contribution to the
philosophical works of India. His other, and most popular,
immortal work of poetry is the Jnaneshwari, a classic commentary
on the Bhagavad Gita. Even today, after 700 years, it has great
influence on the people of Maharashtra; reciting it has become a
part and passion of their culture. A commentary on a book is
naturally limited to the contents of that book, because the
commentator's purpose is to expound on the views of the author.
Therefore, when Jnaneshwar placed the Jnaneshwari at the feet of
his Guru Nivrittinath, who was his own elder brother, the Guru
said, "In this book you have explained what someone else has said.
Now write what you have to say." Thus at the command of his Guru,
Jnaneshwar wrote the Amritanubhava, which exudes the nectarean
sweetness of his own experience of the Self. It is a work of
matchless poetic beauty, profound philosophy and eternal wisdom.

Jnaneshwar declares that nothing is false or illusory;
rather, everything is the play of Consciousness. The world is
in God. In fact, the world is God. It is the expression of God's
divine love, which is His own power, or Shakti, not separate from
Him, from which the world spontaneously manifests. So God is
love, and divine love is nectarean. Therefore the experience
(anubhava) of the taste of that nectar (amrit) is the experience
of God, of Self, of immortality.

In the Amritanubhava, Jnaneshwar has performed the great
task of describing this indescribable experience. The words of a
Siddha can be fully understood only by another Siddha who shares
the same experience. But others, who have received the grace of
the Guru, can get a glimpse of the unfathomable depth and
immeasurable height of the wisdom behind those words. Those who
have an interest in this book, who become intoxicated by it and
whose mouths water from its taste are indeed fortunate; they are
worthy of receiving its knowledge.

Jnaneshwar was not only a great saint but also a great poet, whose lofty imagination gave expression to a wealth of images and analogies which he put in the simple Marathi language of the people of that time. He was not only a philosopher, but also a Siddha yogi with divine experience. He had that perfect blend of knowledge (jnana), devotion (bhakti) and yoga. Above all, he was a great lover of the Guru, whom he regarded as the source of all his achievements--literary, yogic and spiritual. His words are a flowing stream of divine inspiration, an outcome of his own experience. This makes him bold enough, at one point, to say with confidence, "It is not that we accept this merely because it was said by Lord Shiva or Lord Krishna. It can be understood even if they had not said it." Only Beings like Baba can fully appreciate such a statement. The experience of the eternal Truth is the same at all times. One who has experienced it can recognize it in another, just as one who has fallen in love knows the joyous state of one who is in love.

After I read Jnaneshwar I understood Baba's love for him. I could find no difference in their teachings. Baba's teaching is confirmed by Jnaneshwar's. The inseparable union of Shiva and Shakti, the divine knowledge and love of the Guru, the sole existence of the Self, the nonexistence of ignorance, the awakening of the awakened, the natural state of Self-awareness, and other subtle mysteries of spiritual experience are what Jnaneshwar shares in the Amritanubhava and what Baba also shares in his Play of Consciousness. Both Baba and Jnaneshwar belong to the Siddha tradition. They are graduates of the same university and members of the same faculty. Therefore, their philosophy, teaching and experience do not differ. The words of the Amritanubhava may as well be Baba's words.

When Baba pays his respects to Jnaneshwar at his samadhi shrine, he looks to me like a 71-year-old younger brother visiting his 21-year-old elder brother. As Baba sits there quietly near Jnaneshwar's altar stone, he appears to be communicating with Jnaneshwar, who is also sitting there, below the altar. They seem to be silently comparing notes and agreeing that words are useless to describe That; that the form and the formless are but one God; that the Guru is the means to God; and that since there is no bondage, practicing spiritual disciplines is like trying to get rid of what does not exist. Thus, they seem like two lamps emitting one light. One is the bliss of freedom, the other the bliss of knowledge--but the bliss is the same. They seem to enjoy each other's company, sharing the knowledge of God and the mysteries of the universe.

Each line of the Amritanubhava is full of such deep meaning that it is not easy to fully grasp its sublime philosophy. There are more than ten commentaries to explain its verses, but not too many translations. No other language can totally capture the homey words, naive expressions and poetic rhetoric that give even the original unliterary Marathi language a richness of form and depth of content. Those words stir the heart and awaken one from an age-long slumber to alert awareness. Words generally wear out with time, but the words which Jnaneshwar left behind have become a timeless wonder through the touch of his divine love.

At the end of the book Jnaneshwar himself says that he wrote the Amritanubhava out of love for the Self. Otherwise there was no need to write about That which is self-revealing. Who needs a flashlight to see the self-illuminating sun? He says that he has not given out a secret. The Self would not remain unexposed even if he were to keep silent about it. Words and silence are the same for the Self. So why not write? He writes out of love for That though it is self-evident. Though tasted before, a nectarean drink always gives new delight when tasted again. Even liberated beings yearn to drink it. Jnaneshwar does not want to enjoy it only by himself. The sun is given light to shine on all. Clouds are given water to shower on earth. He too wants to share with all his experience which was given by his Guru. Jnaneshwar urges us to enjoy the feast he offers. Just as all metals, base or purified, turn to gold at the touch of the philosopher's stone, so also whoever, high or low, sips of this nectar of self-awareness will become one with the Self, with Shiva.

The Amritanubhava is the embodiment in words of the formless divine Truth. Therefore, its words penetrate into the innermost recesses of the heart, the seat of the Divine.

Jnaneshwar speaks of things that are too sublime and subtle to be expressed in words; but what is important is what the words embody, not just the language. Even if we were to get only a glimpse of That to which his words refer, it will ultimately expand our vision.

Swami Abhayananda, himself a poet, has done a fine job of rendering the Amritanubhava into English as the Nectar of Self-Awareness. He has made the text clearer for us. He has also rendered into beautiful English two other short but sublime works of Jnaneshwar, Haripath and Changdev Pasasthi, which are included at the end of this book.

However subtle the subject matter of this book may be, I am sure that those who have received Baba's grace and teaching will not only understand it, but relish it with great joy, becoming established in the bliss of Self-awareness.

Let Jnaneshwar inspire us and our Guru awaken us to our own true identity.

Swami Prajnananda

AMRITANUBHAV

Introduction To Amritanubhav

Amritanubhav, or The Nectar Of Self-Awareness, is one of the great books of the world. It was written on the instruction of his Guru by one of the most amazing and awe-inspiring saints of India. Jnaneshwar, or Jnanadev, as he sometimes calls himself, was truly the lord of knowledge as his name implies. At the age of fifteen he wrote his famous commentaries on the Bhagavad Gita, called Jnaneshwari, and then afterward wrote this original Marathi masterpiece to give a clear unified expression to the saving knowledge he wished to impart to the world.

At the age of twenty-two, he requested his friends to bury him alive in the tomb in which he remains to this day in the town of Alandi, in Maharashtra. Several hundred years after his burial, another great soul, Eknath Maharaj, received a message in his meditation from Jnaneshwar to dig into his grave and remove the tree root which was growing into the place of his interment. This Eknath did, and found that the body was still alive, still warm, though seemingly in a trance state.

Only Jnanadev knows why he chooses to remain in the body in such a state, but many pilgrims to the shrine of his entombment have testified to the rare efficacy of the atmosphere around that place. Many thousands continue to receive spiritual instructions and blessings from Jnaneshwar, and his shrine has become a holy place, charged with an extremely intense aura of spiritual energy.

Jnanedev's Life

The life of Jnanadev is shrouded in legend. He is said to have been born in 1275 AD in a pious Brahmin family. All of his brothers and his sister also became revered saints; his famous sister Muktabai wrote many devotional songs which are sung in India to this day, and his brother Nivrittinath, who was only two years older, served as his Guru.

Jnanadev is said to have been a Siddha; that is, he had reached the highest possible level of Consciousness, and possessed all the miraculous powers. Many stories are told of miraculous events in the brief life of Jnanadev. One such story relates how a great and powerful, but somewhat proud, sage named Changadeva was coming to pay a visit to Jnanadev, apparently to prove himself the more powerful of the two. And Jnanadev, sitting atop a stone wall with his brothers, spotted Changadeva in the distance riding toward them on a tiger and brandishing a cobra as a whip. Jnanadev exclaimed, "Ah, let's go and meet him!", and with that, he caused the wall with himself and his brothers and sister perched on top to proceed down the road toward Changadeva. Changadeva was naturally put in his place, and humbly acknowledged Jnanadev as his Master.

But the greatest miracles which Jnaneshwar produced -- those which have created the greatest beneficent effect on posterity -- are his two literary products, Jnaneshwari and Amritanubhav. In these two works he fully reveals the highest knowledge that he possesses. Only as a means of categorization may we speak of these two works as 'philosophy'. They are, in actuality, the recorded experience of a great illumined soul.

Besides being not just a philosopher, Jnanadev is also not just an illumined saint. His stature is really unguessable, but if we think for a moment on the ability, which he evidences, to maintain a body in a still position for these many centuries, while presumably operating on subtler levels for the spiritual upliftment of man, we are forced to accord him a unique place in the assembly of those who have attained the knowledge of Reality.

What Jnanadev says, therefore, is certainly worth hearing, and worth contemplating. In Amritanubhav, the Nectar of Self-Awareness, he has set forth a clear and penetrating statement of his vision, and the reader who becomes absorbed in, and thus elevated to the level of, Jnanadev's thought, finds himself on some very giddy heights of awareness. At times Jnanadev's questions and similes bring the mind to the brink of a precipice where it finds itself clawing at thin air. It is then possible to find oneself making the magic leap into the awareness of pure Consciousness. Thus, this book -- though somewhat difficult -- if studied with a one-pointed effort toward comprehension, actually serves as a vehicle for imparting the experience of the Self.

Jnanadev's Philosophy

As 'philosophy', Jnanadev's is the highest non-duality, surpassing even the Vedantic conception of Reality in its insistence on unqualified Unity. Much, in fact, of what Jnanadev has to say in this work is directed toward the Vedantins, or Maya-vadins, as they were sometimes called.

In the world-conception attributed to Shankaracharya and other representatives of Vedanta philosophy, the perception of the existence of the world is attributed to ignorance, or ajnana; and once this ignorance is removed, one is able to see that there is nothing but the unembodied Absolute, the one undifferentiated pure Consciousness. Often the analogy of a rope appearing as a snake is used: The appearance is unreal; it is caused by ignorance. But once this ignorance is dispelled, the Reality is seen, and it is perceived that there never was a snake but only the rope all along.

Well, Jnanadev takes issue with this line of thinking, and states emphatically that there is no such thing as ignorance; that even this multitude of sense objects is only that Being, the one Self, and that the perception of it, far from being caused by ignorance, is caused by the Lord's delight in perceiving Himself. In short, there is no room for anything other than the one Self in Jnanadev's philosophy. There is no place for Maya, or illusion, for he dissolves the barriers which separate the world and God, and his vision refuses to allow any disruption to the Unity that he sees spreading everywhere, whether with his eyes closed in meditation, or awake and active in the manifested world.

Jnanadev's influence has been scarcely felt in the West, but in India it is considerable -- especially in Maharashtra state where many later saints such as Eknath and Tukaram, as well as his contemporary, Namadev, have honored him and expounded on his teaching. This song of his, The Nectar Of Self-Awareness, in an expression of

the philosophy which came to be known as 'Kashmir Shaivism'. It is
a clear and irrefutable exposition of that unparalleled wisdom
which sees nothing but God and which cultivates the conscious
awareness that everything before one's eyes is the delightful
sport of the Self.

    This is the 'Nectar' which Jnanadev proffers for us to sip.
It is a gift for which we have reason to give thanks. To one who
understands, its sweetness is beyond measure. It is, indeed, a
gift of the divine Lord, that through awareness we may take delight
in our own immeasurable Bliss.

                      Swami Abhayananda

AMRITANUBHAV

(The Nectar Of Self-Awareness)

Invocation:

> I take refuge in the God
> Who is known as the glorious Nivrittinath, (1)
> The one indescribable Bliss
> Who is unborn, immortal, and ever-unchanged.
>
> I honor the divine Wisdom
> In the form of the Guru,
> Who, overflowing with compassion,
> Showers his blessings on all,
> And whose commands point the way to victory.
>
> Though one, He appears as Shiva and Shakti. (2)
> Whether is it Shiva joined to Shakti
> Or Shakti joined to Shiva,
> No one can tell.
>
> I bow to these parents of the worlds,
> Who, by revealing to each other their oneness,
> Enable me also to know it.
>
> I make obeisance to Shambhu, (3)
> That perfect Lord who is
> The Cause of the beginning,
> Preservation, and end of the world;
> The Manifestation of the beginning,
> Middle and end of the world;
> And the Dissolution of the three as well.

Chapter One:

The Union Of Shiva And Shakti

1. I offer obeisance to the God and Goddess,
    The limitless primal parents of the universe.

2. The Lover, out of boundless love,
    Has become the beloved.
    Both are made of the same substance
    And share the same food.

3. Out of love for each other, they merge.
    And again they separate for the pleasure of being two.

4. They are not entirely the same --
    Nor are they not the same.
    We cannot say what they really are.

5. Their one great desire is to enjoy themselves.
    Yet they never allow their unity to be disturbed
    Even as a joke.

6. They are so averse to separation
    That even their child, the universe,
    Does not disturb their union.

7. Though they perceive the universe
    Of inanimate and animate creation
    Emanating from themselves,
    They do not recognize a third.

8. They sit together on the same ground,
    Wearing the same garment of light.
    From time past remembrance they have lived thus --
    United in Bliss.

9. Difference itself merged in their sweet union
    When, seeing their intimacy,
    It could find no duality to enjoy.

10. Because of God, the Goddess exists,
    And without Her, He is not.
    They exist only because of each other.

11. How sweet is their union!
    The whole world is too small to contain them,
    Yet they live happily in the smallest particle.

12. They regard each other as their own Self,
    And neither creates so much as a blade
    Of grass without the other.

13. These two are the only ones
    Who dwell in this home called the universe.
    When the Master of the house sleeps,
    The Mistress stays awake,
    And performs the function of both.

14. When He awakes, the whole house disappears,
    And nothing is left.

15. They became two for the purpose of diversity;
    And both are seeking each other
    For the purpose of becoming One.

16. Each is an object to the other.
    And both are subjects to each other.
    Only when together do they enjoy happiness.

17. It is Shiva alone who lives in all forms;
    He is both the male and the female.
    It is because of the union of these two halves
    That the whole universe exists.

18. Two lutes -- one note.
    Two flowers -- one fragrance.
    Two lamps -- one light.

19. Two lips -- one word.
    Two eyes -- one sight.
    These two -- one universe.

20. Though manifesting duality,
    These two -- the eternal pair --
    Are eating from the same dish.

21. The Shakti, endowed with chastity and fidelity,
    Cannot live without Her Lord.
    And without Her,
    The Doer-of-all cannot be.

22. Since He appears because of Her,
    And She exists because of Her Lord,
    The two cannot be distinguished at all.

23. Sugar and its sweetness
    Cannot be told apart,
    Nor camphor and its fragrance.

24. If we have the flames,
    We have also the fire.
    If we catch hold of Shakti,
    We have Shiva as well.

25. The Sun appears to shine because of its rays --
    But the rays themselves are produced by the Sun.
    In fact, that glorious Sun and its shining
    Are the same.

26. To have a reflection, one must have an object.
    If we see a reflection, then we infer that
    An object exists.
    Likewise, the supreme Reality which is One
    Appears to be two.

27. Through Her,
    The absolute Void became the primal Person;
    And She derived Her existence from Her Lord.

28. Shiva formed His beloved Himself;
    And without Her presence,
    No Person exists.

29. Because of Her form,
    God is seen in the world.
    Yet it was He
    Who created Her form of Himself.

30. Embarrassed by Her formless Husband
    And Her own graceful form,
    She adorned Him with a universe
    Of myriad names and forms.

31. In unity, there is little to behold.
    But She, of good fortune,
    Brought forth the world as a play.

32. She made evident the glory of Her Lord
    By spreading out Her own body-form.
    And He made Her famous by concealing Himself.

33. He takes the role of Witness
    Out of love of watching Her.
    But if He cannot see Her,
    He abandons Himself as well.

34. Because of Her,
    He assumes the form of the universe.
    Without Her,
    He is left naked.

35. Although He is manifest,
    He cannot be seen.
    It is only by Her grace
    That He appears as universal form.

36. When He is awakened by Her,
    Shiva perceives the world.
    Then He enjoys this dish She serves,
    As well as She who serves.

37. While He sleeps, She gives birth
    To the animate and inanimate worlds.
    When She rests,
    Her husband disappears.

38. When He conceals Himself,
    He cannot be discovered without Her grace.
    They are as mirrors, each to the other.

39. When He embraces Her,
    It is His own bliss that Shiva enjoys.
    He is the Enjoyer of everything,
    But there is no enjoyment without Her.

40. She is His form,
    But Her beauty comes from Him.
    By their intermingling,
    They are together enjoying this feast.

41. Shiva and Shakti are the same,
    Like air and its motion,
    Or gold and its lustre.

42. Fragrance cannot be separated from musk,
    Nor heat from fire;
    Neither can Shakti be separated from Shiva.

43. If night and day were to approach the Sun,
    Both would disappear.
    In the same way, their duality would vanish
    If their essential Unity were seen.

44. In fact,
    Shiva and Shakti are ever averse
    To the primal unitive state
    From which AUM emanates.

45. Jnanadev says,
    "I honor the primal pair of Shiva and Shakti
    Who, by partaking of the sweet dish of name and form,
    Shed light on the Essence which supports them."

46. Embracing each other, they merge into one,
    As darkness and light at the breaking of dawn.

47. All levels of speech, from <u>Para</u> to <u>Vaikari</u>, (1)
    Merge into silence
    When their true nature is realized,
    Just as the ocean and the Ganges both merge
    Into the primal waters
    When the time of Dissolution comes.

48. The air along with its motion merges
    Into the universal air;
    The Sun along with its brilliance merges
    In the elemental fire at that time.

49.   Likewise, while attempting
      To see Shiva and Shakti,
      Both the seer and his vision disappear.
      Again and again I offer salutations
      To that universal pair.

50.   They are like a stream of knowledge
      From which a knower cannot drink
      Unless he gives up himself.

51.   When such is the case,
      If I remain separate in order to honor them,
      It is only a pretended separation.

52.   My homage is like that
      Of a golden ornament
      Worshipping gold.

53.   When my tongue says the word, 'tongue',
      Is there any difference between the
      Organ which utters the word
      And the object it represents?

54.   Although the names, 'Ganges' and 'ocean' are different,
      When they commingle,
      Are their waters not the same?

55.   The Sun is both the source
      And the object of illumination;
      Still it is only one.

56.   If moonlight illumines the moon,
      Or if a lamp is revealed by the light of itself,
      Is there any separation here?

57.   When the lustre of a pearl
      Plays upon itself,
      It only enhances itself.

58.   Is the sound of AUM divided into three
      Simply because it contains three letters?
      Or is the letter 'N' divided into three
      Because of the three lines by which it is formed?

59.   So long as Unity is undisturbed,
      And a graceful pleasure is thereby derived,
      Why should not the water find delight
      In the floral fragrance of its rippled surface?

60.   It is in this manner I bow
      To the inseparable Shiva and Shakti.

61. A reflected image merges with its object
    When the mirror is taken away.
    When the air is still, the ripples vanish.

62. A man comes to himself
    When he wakes from sleep.
    Likewise, I have perceived the God and Goddess
    By waking from my ego.

63. When salt dissolves,
    It becomes one with the ocean;
    When my ego dissolved,
    I became one with Shiva and Shakti.

64. I have paid homage to Shiva and Shakti
    By uniting with them --
    Just as the inner space of the plantain tree (2)
    Is united with the space outside
    When its outer covering is removed.

*   *   *

Chapter Two:

Salutations To Sri Nivrittinath

1. Now I offer salutations to Him
   Who is the well-spring to the garden of sadhana,
   The auspicious thread of divine Will,
   And, though formless,
   The very incarnation of compassion.

2. I offer salutations to Him
   Who comes to the aid of the Self
   Which is suffering limitation
   In the wilderness of ignorance.

3. I bow to my Guru, Nivritti, (1)
   Who, by slaying the elephant of Maya,
   Has made a dish of the pearls
   Taken from its temple.

4. By his mere glance,
   Bondage becomes liberation,
   And the Knower becomes the known.

5. He distributes the gold of liberation to all,
   Both the great and the small;
   It is He who gives the vision of the Self.

6. As for his powers,
   He surpasses even the greatness of Shiva.
   He is a mirror in which the Self
   Sees the reflection of its own bliss.

7. It is by his grace
   That all the moon-phases of sadhana
   Culminate in the full moon of realization.

8. All the sadhaka's efforts cease
   When he meets the Guru.
   He is the ocean in which the river
   Of activity has ceased to be.

9. When he is absent,
   One wears the lovely cloak of appearance.
   When he appears,
   The cloak of diversity vanishes.

10. The Sun of his grace turns the darkness of ignorance
    Into the light of self-knowledge.

11. The water of his grace
    Washes the soul so clean
    That he regards even Shiva as unclean,
    And does not wish to be touched
    Even by him.

12. He abandoned the greatness of his own state
    To save his disciple,
    Yet his true greatness has never been abandoned.

13. Alone, there is no happiness.
    Therefore, the pure Consciousness
    Assumes the forms of Guru and disciple.

14. By just a little sprinkle of his grace,
    The poison of ignorance is changed into nectar --
    The nectar of limitless knowledge.

15. When knowledge discovers him within,
    He swallows up the knower;
    And still he does not become impure.

16. With his help
    The soul attains the state of Brahman,
    But if he is indifferent,
    Brahman has no more worth than a blade of grass.

17. Those who faithfully endeavor,
    Regarding his will as law,
    Obtain the ripe fruit of their efforts.

18. Unless the well-spring of his glance
    Waters the garden of knowledge,
    There will be no fruit in the hand.

19. By casting a mere glance,
    He makes the world of appearance
    Recede and vanish.
    Though his conquest is great,.
    He does not call it his own.

20. He has attained the great status of 'Guru'
    By possessing no status.
    His wealth is his ability
    To rid us of what does not exist.

21. He is the rock of refuge
    Which saves us from drowning
    In the sea which does not exist.
    Those who are saved are
    Released from time and space.

22. He is like the ever-perfect inner sky.
    To that, the outer sky cannot compare.

23. From his light,
    The moon with her cool beams is made;
    The Sun derives its brilliance
    From a single ray of his light.

24. He is like an astrologer whom Shiva,
    weary of assuming individual forms,
    Has commissioned to find an auspicious time
    For the regaining of his own state.

25. He is like the moon whose form
    Is not diminished, but enhanced,
    By the wearing of a gown of light.

26. Though present, he is not seen.
    Though he is light, he does not illumine.
    Though he always is, he is not in any place.

27. How much more shall I say,
    Using the words, 'he' and 'who'?
    He cannot be explained by words.

28. He is indescribable.
    In his unity, where there is no duality,
    Words become silent.

29. The object of Knowledge reveals itself
    When the means of knowledge ceases to be.
    It is this non-being which he loves the most.

30. Though we may wish to have a glimpse of him,
    Even that seeing, in his kingdom,
    Is a stain.

31. When such is the case,
    How could one find entrance to his kingdom
    By means of praise or by reference to him?
    Even his name becomes merged in him!

32. The Self does not seek himself.
    Neither does he fly from himself.
    He merely retains a name
    To serve as a veil.

33. How can he destroy what does not exist?
    How can he be called the Destroyer?

34. The Sun is called the destroyer of darkness,
    But when did the Sun perceive any darkness?

35. That which is illusory becomes real;
    That which is inanimate becomes animate,
    And that which is impossible becomes possible
    Through his marvelous sport.

36. Through your wondrous power, you create illusions --
    And then reject them as mere illusions.
    You remain beyond the illusions;
    You are not the object of any kind of vision.

37. O Satguru, you are so mysterious!
    How then am I to treat of you?
    You do not allow yourself to be defined by words.

38. You have created so many names and forms,
    And destroyed them again through your power,
    Yet still you are not satisfied.

39. You do not give your friendship to anyone
    Without taking away his sense of individuality.

40. If one tries to attach a name to him,
    Even the name, 'Self' does not fit.
    He refuses to be confined to a particular thing.

41. To the Sun, there is no night;
    In water, there is no salt;
    To one who is awake, there is no sleep.

42. In the presence of fire, camphor cannot remain;
    In his presence, name and form cease to be.

43. Though I try to bow to him,
    He does not remain before me
    As an object of my worship.
    He does not allow any sense of difference.

44. The Sun does not become something else
    In order to serve as a means for its rising.
    Neither does he become an object for my worship.

45. By no means may one place oneself before him;
    He has removed the possibility
    Of his being an object of anyone's worship.

46. If you mirror the sky,
    There is seen no reflection.
    Neither is he an object
    Which someone may worship.

47. So what if he is not an object of worship!
    Why should it seem so mysterious to me?
    But he does not leave any trace
    Of the one who goes to worship!

48. When the outside of a garment is opened,
    The inside is opened as well.

49. Or, as a mirrored image must vanish
When the object of reflection is gone,
So must the one who worships vanish
When the object of worship disappears.

50. Our vision is worthless where there is no form.
We are placed in such a state
By the grace of his feet.

51. The flame of a lamp is kept burning continually
By the combination of the wick and the oil;
A piece of camphor cannot keep it burning.

52. For as soon as the camphor and flame are united,
Both of them vanish at once.

53. When he is seen,
Both worshipper and the object of worship vanish
As dreams at the moment of waking.

54. By these verses I have made a finish of duality,
And also honored my beloved Sri Guru.

55. How wonderful is his friendship!
He has manifested duality
In the form of Guru and disciple
Where there is not even a place for one!

56. How does he have a close relationship with himself
When there is no one other than himself?
He can never become anything other than himself!

57. He becomes as vast as the sky,
Including the entire universe within himself.
Within him
Even darkness and non-existence dwell.

58. An ocean fulfills the needs of all,
Yet it cannot be fulfilled itself.
Also in the Guru's house
Such contradictions happily live.

59. There is no intimacy between night and day --
But they are one in the eyes of the Sun.

60. Although the supreme Reality is one,
Differences arise within It.
How does differentiation detract
From the unity of the Whole?
Does the existence of opposites within contradict
The unity of the Whole?

61. The words, 'Guru' and 'disciple'
    Refer to but one;
    The Guru alone exists as both these forms.

62. Gold alone exists in both gold and in ornaments.
    The moon alone exists in both moon and in moonlight.

63. Camphor and its fragrance are nothing but camphor.
    Sugar and its sweetness are nothing but sugar.

64. Although Guru and disciple appear as two,
    It is Guru alone who masquerades as both.

65. When you look in a mirror and see your own face,
    You know it is only yourself.

66. If a person awakes in a solitary place
    When no one else is about,
    Then one may be sure that he is both
    The awakened and the awakener as well.

67. Just as the awakened and awakener are the same,
    The Guru is both the receiver of knowledge
    And the one who imparts it as well.
    In this way he upholds the relationship
    Between the Master and the disciple.

68. If one could see his own eye without a mirror,
    There would be no need of this sport of the Guru.

69. Therefore he nourishes this intimate relationship
    Without causing duality or disturbing the unity.

70. His name is Nivritti.
    Nivritti is his splendor.
    Nivritti is the glory of his kingdom.

71. He is not the 'nivritti'
    Which means the cessation of action;

72. That nivritti is the product of
    Pravritti, or action --
    Just as night is necessitated
    By its opposite, day.
    He is not this 'nivritti'.

73. He is the pure and supreme Lord;
    He is not the kind of jewel
    Which needs something else
    To cause it to sparkle.

74. The moon spreads its soft light,
    Pervading the entire sky.
    It is she herself who
    Enhances her own form.

75. Likewise, Nivritti is the cause of Nivritti.
    He is like a flower become a nose
    In order to enjoy its own fragrance.

76. Would a mirror be needed
    If one's vision were able to turn back on itself
    And perceive the fairness of one's own complexion?

77. Though night dissolves and daylight comes,
    Is not the Sun unchanged,
    Without the need to make an effort
    To return to himself?

78. Nivritti is not an object of knowledge
    Which requires various proofs
    To show it exists;
    There is no doubt that he is the Guru.

79. Salutations to the holy feet of Guru
    Whose actionlessness is absolute
    Without any trace of action.

80. Jnanadeva says, "This salutation to Sri Guru
    Satisfies the requirements
    Of all the four levels of speech."

*   *   *

Chapter Three:

The Requirements Of Speech

1. It is the calling aloud of these four levels of speech
   Which awakens the Self.
   But even this waking is a kind of sleep.

2. It is true that these four levels of speech
   Are conducive to soul-liberation,
   But with the destruction of ignorance,
   These also are destroyed.

3. Just as hands and feet depart along with the body
   At the time of death,
   Or as the subtle senses depart along with the mind,
   Or as the Sun's rays depart with the setting Sun,

4. Or as dreams depart when sleep comes to an end,
   So the four levels of speech depart
   Along with ignorance.

5. When iron is burned, it continues to exist as liquid;
   Fuel burnt continues as fire.

6. Salt dissolved in water
   Continues to exist as taste;
   Sleep dispelled continues as wakefulness.

7. In the same way, although the four levels of speech
   Are destroyed along with ignorance,
   They continue to live as knowledge of Reality.

8. It's true, they light the lamp of knowledge
   Through their sacrifice,
   But this kind of knowledge is a futile exertion.

9. Sleep, while it remains,
   Is the cause of one's dreams;
   And when it vanishes,
   It causes the individual to become awake to himself.
   It is sleep that is the cause of both.

10. In the same way,
    Ignorance -- while it remains --
    Is the cause of false knowledge,
    And when it vanishes,
    Is the cause of true knowledge.

11. But, living or dead,
    This ignorance entangles the individual
    By binding him
    With either slavery or so-called 'freedom'.

12. If freedom itself is a kind of bondage,
    Why should the word 'freedom' be given to it?

13. A child is satisfied
    By the death of an ogre in a dream.
    But it does not even exist for others!
    How should they be affected by its death?

14. If someone bewails
    The loss of a broken vase which never existed,
    Would we consider that person wise?

15. If bondage itself is unreal,
    How can real freedom arise from its destruction?
    This freedom is only something created
    By the self-destruction of ignorance.

16. Sadashiva,
    In the Shiva Sutras,
    Has declared that knowledge itself is bondage.

17. It is not that we accept this
    Merely because it was said by Shiva or by Krishna.
    It can be understood
    Even if they had not said it.

18. Sri Krishna (in the Bhagavad Gita)
    Has elaborately explained how
    The quality of Satva binds one
    With the cords of knowledge.

19. If the Self, which is pure Knowledge itself,
    Requires the help of another knowledge,
    Would that not be like the Sun seeking help
    Of another light?

20. It is meaningless to say
    That the Self is itself Knowledge
    If its greatness depends
    On some knowledge other than itself.
    If a lamp desires another lamp
    To give it light,
    It must be that it has gone out.

21. Could one who was ignorant of his own existence
    Wander about to various countries in search of himself?

22. How might one declare
    That he was happy to remember himself
    After so many days?

23. Also, if the Self,
    Who is himself pure Consciousness,
    Thinks, "I am conscious of myself -- I am He!",
    Such knowledge would be bondage.

24. This kind of knowledge is deplorable
    Since it conceals the original knowledge
    And fosters the illusion of freedom.

25. Therefore,
    When the ego of the individual is destroyed,
    And ignorance vanishes,
    The four levels of speech --
    Which are ornaments of the four bodies --
    Also vanish.

26. When ignorance, being utterly dejected,
    Enters the fire of Consciousness
    Along with her organs,
    Nothing remains but the ashes of knowledge.

27. When camphor is dissolved in water,
    It cannot be seen,
    But can be detected as fragrance in the water.

28. When ashes are smeared on the body,
    The loose particles may fall away,
    But the white coloration remains.

29. Even though the water of a river
    May have ceased to flow,
    Still it remains in the moisture of the soil.

30. Though one's shadow may not be seen at noontime,
    Still it remains under one's feet.

31. So also the knowing
    That swallows everything other than itself
    Is merged in the ultimate Reality,
    But remains as knowing.

32. The requirements of the four levels of speech
    Cannot be satisfied even by their self-sacrifice.
    I have satisfied them by bowing my head
    At the holy feet of the Guru.

33. When the four levels of speech are destroyed,
    They cling to that knowledge
    Which is itself a kind of ignorance.

*   *   *

Chapter Four:

Knowledge And Ignorance

1. By destroying ignorance,
   Knowledge reigns supreme
   Like the wakefulness that destroys sleep.

2. By looking in a mirror, one perceives his own identity --
   But that identity was already there.

3. In the same way, knowledge gives the understanding
   Of the identity of the world and the Self --
   But it is like using a knife
   To cut another knife.

4. If a person enters a house,
   And then sets it on fire,
   He gets burned along with the house.
   If a thief gets into a sack
   And then fastens it shut,
   He is bound along with the sack.

5. Fire,
   In the process of burning the camphor,
   Burns itself up as well.
   This is also what happens to knowledge
   In the process of destroying ignorance.

6. When the support of ignorance is taken away,
   Knowledge spreads,
   To the extent that it destroys itself.

7. As the wick of an oil-lamp burns to its end,
   The flame flares up more brightly than before.
   But this brightness
   Is nothing but its extinction.

8. Is the breast of a woman rising or falling?
   Is the jasmine bud blooming or fading?
   Who can say?

9. The rise of a wave is but its fall;
   The flash of a bolt of lightning
   Is but its fading.

10. Likewise, knowledge,
    Drinking up the water of ignorance,
    Grows so large
    That it completely annihilates itself.

11. When the final deluge occurs,
    It engulfs all water and all space,
    And leaves nothing outside of it.

12. Then, also,
    The disc of the Sun becomes larger than the universe,
    And both darkness and light merge
    In that pure Light.

13. Then,
    After destroying sleep,
    Wakefulness destroys itself,
    And remains in its state of pure Consciousness.

14. In the same way,
    That knowledge which shines
    By virtue of the existence of ignorance,
    Is swallowed up by absolute Knowledge.

15. This absolute Knowledge is like
    A moon which neither waxes nor wanes.

16. The only thing one might compare it to
    Is the Sun,
    Which is never overpowered by any other luminary
    Nor ever cast into darkness.

17. For pure Consciousness also
    Is not enlightened by another kind of knowledge
    Or darkened by ignorance.

18. But can pure Consciousness be conscious of itself?
    Can the eyeball perceive itself?

19. Can the sky enter the sky?
    Can fire burn fire?
    Can a person climb onto his own head?

20. Can vision perceive itself?
    Does taste have its own taste?
    Can sound listen to itself?

21. Can the Sun illumine itself?
    Can a fruit bear fruit?
    Can fragrance smell itself?

22. Just as these things are not possible,
    Neither is pure Consciousness
    Conscious of itself.
    For it does not have the quality of 'being conscious'.

23. If knowledge requires the aid
    Of some other knowledge,
    It is nothing but ignorance.

24. What is light is not darkness --
    But is it an illumination to itself?

25. In the same way,
    He neither is nor is not.
    By saying this,
    It seems that I'm saying 'He is not'.

26. But then, if that were true --
    That nothing is --
    Who knows that there is nothing?

27. By what grounds may one prove
    The theory of Nihilism?
    It is a totally unjustified imputation
    To the ultimate Reality.

28. If the extinguisher of light
    Is extinguished along with the light,
    Who is it who knows that there is no light?

29. If one ceases to be
    During the period of sleep,
    Who is it who knows that it was a nice sleep?

30. Let us take a pot.
    If it is broken, its brokeness is perceived.
    But if it does not exist at all,
    Who is it who says it does not exist?

31. Therefore, it can be seen
    That he who perceives that there is nothing,
    Does not himself become nothing.
    The Self has a unique sort of existence,
    Beyond being and non-being.

32. The ultimate Reality
    Is neither an object to itself
    Nor is it an object to any one else.
    Should it then be regarded as non-existent?

33. A person may fall asleep in a remote forest,
    Unperceived by anyone else.
    Since he is asleep,
    He is not conscious of himself either.

34. Still, he does not become lifeless --
    Without existence.
    Pure Existence is like this.
    It does not fit the conception of existence
    Or non-existence.

35. When the vision is turned inward,
    It no longer perceives outside objects,
    But it does not therefore cease to exist
    And to be aware.

36. A very dark-skinned person
     May stand in pitch-darkness.
     Neither he nor anyone else
     May be able to perceive him.
     Still, he knows himself to exist
     Without any doubt.

37. His existence or non-existence
     Is not like that of a person.
     He exists in Himself in His own way.

38. When the sky is clear of clouds,
     It is without form.
     One who looks may see no form,
     But still the sky is there.

39. The crystal-clear water in a tank appears not to be.
     Though one who looks may not see it,
     Still it is there.

40. Thus the ultimate Reality
     Exists as Existence,
     And is beyond the concepts of 'is' and 'is not'.

41. It is like the awakeness that exists
     When there is no remembrance
     Of the sleep that has vanished,
     Nor remembrance of its own being.

42. When a jar is placed on the ground,
     It is called the ground with a jar.
     When the jar is taken away,
     It is called the ground without a jar.

43. But when neither of these conditions exists,
     The ground remains in its pure state.
     The existence of the ultimate Reality is like this.

*   *   *

Chapter Five:

Existence, Consciousness, Bliss

1. These three attributes, Sat, Chit, and Ananda
    (Existence, Consciousness and Bliss),
    Do not actually define Brahman.
    What is poison to others is not poison to itself.

2. Shininess, hardness, and yellowness,
    Together signify gold;
    Stickiness, sweetness, and thickness,
    Together signify honey.

3. Whiteness, fragrance, and softness,
    Are not three separate things,
    But only camphor.

4. Camphor is white;
    Not only that, but it is soft;
    And not only this, it is fragrant as well.

5. Just as these three qualities signify
    One object -- camphor -- and not three objects,
    So the three qualities,
    Sat, Chit, and Ananda,
    Are contained in one Reality.

6. It is true that the words,
    'Sat', 'Chit', and 'Ananda',
    Are different,
    But the three are united in one Bliss.

7. Sat is Ananda and Chit --
    Or is it that Chit is Sat and Ananda?
    They cannot be separated --
    Just as sweetness cannot be separated from honey.

8. The moon in the sky appears to pass through
    Increasing stages of fullness,
    But the moon is always the same;
    It is always full.

9. When water is falling in drops,
    We can count them.
    But when the water is gathered
    In a puddle on the ground,
    It is impossible to count the number of drops.

10. In the same way,
The scriptures describe Reality
As Sat, or Existence,
In order to negate its non-existence.
They call It Chit, or Consciousness,
In order to negate its lack of consciousness.

11. The Vedas,
Which are the very breath of the Lord,
Declare It to be Ananda, or Bliss,
In order to negate the possibility
Of pain existing in It.

12. 'Non-existence' is merely the counterpart,
Or opposite, of 'existence'.
The latter word is used
Only to differentiate it from the former.

13. Thus, the word, 'Satchidananda',
Used to refer to the Self,
Does not really describe Its nature,
But merely signifies
That It is not the opposite of this.

14. Can those objects which are illumined
By the Sun
Illumine the Sun himself?

15. How, then, could the organ of speech illumine
That by the light of which
That organ itself knows its objects?

16. What means of knowledge would be useful
To the self-illuminating Self
Who is not an object of anyone's knowledge
And Who has no ability to know?

17. The means of knowledge is limited
By the object of knowledge.
It has no use in the case of That
Which is self-evident.

18. The fact is, if we try to know That,
The knowledge itself is That.
How, then, could the knowledge
And the known remain separate?

19. So, the words, 'Sat', 'Chit', and 'Ananda',
Do not denote That;
They are merely inventions of our thought.

20. These well-known words, 'Chit', 'Sat', and 'Ananda',
    Are popularly used, it is true --
    But when the knower becomes
    One with That to which they refer,

21. Then they vanish
    Like the clouds that pour down as rain,
    Or like the rivers which flow into the sea,
    Or like a path when it reaches its goal.

22. A flower fades
    After it gives birth to the fruit;
    The fruit is gone
    After it gives up its juice;
    And the juice is gone
    After it gives satisfaction.

23. A hand is drawn back
    After the offering of oblations;
    A melody ends after giving enjoyment.

24. A mirror is put aside
    After showing to a face its reflection;
    And a person leaves
    After having awakened one who is asleep.

25. Similarly, these three,
    Chit, Sat, and Ananda,
    After awaking the seer to his Self,
    Disappear into silence.

26. Whatever may be said about Him --
    He is not that.
    It is not possible to speak about His real nature,
    Just as it is impossible
    For one to measure himself
    By taking the measurement of his shadow.

27. For when the measurer
    Becomes conscious of himself,
    He feels ashamed,
    And gives up trying to measure himself
    By his shadow.

28. Of course, existence cannot be non-existence.
    But can such existence be called Existence?

29. Can that which has become conscious
    By destroying unconsciousness
    Truly be called Consciousness?

30. In perfect Wakefulness
    There is neither sleeping nor waking.
    Likewise, there is no consciousness
    In pure Consciousness.

31. In perfect bliss,
    There is no feeling of unhappiness.
    But can it, for that reason, be called <u>Bliss</u>?

32. Existence vanishes along with non-existence,
    Consciousness along with unconsciousness,
    And bliss along with misery.
    In the end, nothing remains.

33. Discarding the veil of duality
    And all the pairs of opposites,
    <u>That</u> alone remains
    In its own blessed state.

34. If we count it as one,
    It appears to be something other
    Than the one who counts.
    Not from the viewpoint of enumeration,
    But from the absolute viewpoint,
    It is One.

35. If It were able
    To remain something other than bliss,
    It could enjoy bliss.
    But since It is Itself Bliss,
    How can it enjoy?

36. When the drum of the Goddess is beaten
    She enters the body of the worshipper as sound.
    But when there is no worshipper,
    That sound of beating
    Does not then enter itself.

37. Likewise, He, being Bliss Himself,
    Cannot experience His bliss.
    And, for the same reason,
    He is not aware that He cannot.

38. If a face does not look into the mirror,
    There is neither a face before it
    Nor behind it.
    Likewise, He is neither happiness nor misery,
    But pure Bliss Itself.

39. Abandoning all so-called illuminating concepts
    As but jabberings in a dream,
    He conceals Himself
    From even His own understanding.

40. Even before the sugar cane is planted,
    The juice is within it --
    But its sweetness is known only to itself.

41. Even before the strings of the Vina are plucked,
    The sound is within it --
    But that sound is known only to itself.

42. If a flower wished to enter into itself
    In order to enjoy its own fragrance,
    It would have to become a bee.

43. Only the flavor itself knows
    The flavor of food which is yet to be cooked.

44. So, can That, which does not even enjoy
    Its own blissfulness,
    Be tasted or enjoyed by others?

45. When the moon is overhead at noontime,
    Her presence is known only to herself.

46. It is like beauty before it is given form,
    Or youth before the birth of the body,
    Or religious merit prior to any good action;

47. Or sexual desire before it becomes
    Physically evident as tumescence;

48. Or the talk about
    The sound of a musical instrument
    Which is not yet constructed,
    And so is known only to the sound itself;

49. Or as fire
    Which has not yet known the contact of fuel
    But only the contact of itself.

50. Only those who are able to perceive
    Their own face without a mirror
    Are capable of understanding
    The secret of the self-evident Reality.

51. Such talk as this
    Is like discussing the harvest in storage
    Before the seeds have been sown.

52. Pure Consciousness is beyond
    Both generalizations and particular statements,
    Ever content in Itself.

53. After such a discourse,
    That speech is wise
    Which drinks deeply of silence.

54. It can be seen
    That the various methods of proof
    Have accepted their own unprovability,
    And analogies have solemnly declared
    Their inability to represent the Reality.

55. The various arguments have dissolved themselves
     Because of their own invalidity.
     The assembly of definitions has also dispersed.

56. All of the various means,
     Having proved futile, have departed.
     And the experience itself
     Has abandoned its object.

57. Thought, along with its intent,
     Has died --
     Like a courageous warrior
     In the cause of his master --

58. And understanding,
     Ashamed of its own mode of knowing,
     Has committed suicide.
     The experience -- abandoned to itself alone --
     Is like one beaten and crippled in battle.

59. When the crust
     Of a piece of talc is peeled off,
     The talc itself disappears.

60. If a plaintain tree, troubled by the heat,
     Casts off its outer layers,
     How shall it stand erect?

61. Experience depends on the existence
     Of the experienced and the experiencer.
     When both of these vanish,
     Can the experience alone experience itself?

62. Of what use are words
     When even the experience
     Dissolves itself in this way?

63. How can words describe the supreme Reality
     Where even the subtlest speech itself disappears
     And there is left no trace of sound?

64. Why should there be any talk
     About waking a person who is already awake?
     Does one begin to cook his food
     After he has taken his meal and become satisfied?

65. When the Sun rises,
     The light of the lamps is not needed.
     Is there a need for a plough
     At the time of harvest?

66. There is no cause of bondage and freedom.
     There is nothing to be accomplished.
     There is only the pleasure of expounding.

                    *   *   *

Chapter Six:

Inefficacy Of The Word

1.   When something is forgotten,
     Either by ourselves or by another,
     We are reminded of it by the word
     Which we use to represent it.

2.   If it had no other glory than this, however,
     The word would not have so much value.

3.   But the word,
     Which -- as everyone knows --
     Serves as a reminder,
     Is, in fact, a very useful thing.
     Is it not a mirror which reflects
     What has no form?

4.   It is no great wonder that what is visible
     May be seen in a mirror,
     But in the mirror of the word,
     What is invisible may be seen.

5.   What the rising Sun is to the sky,
     The word is to the sky of the Infinite.
     The sky is as it is
     Through the power of the word.

6.   The word is the flower
     Of the sky of the Infinite;
     Its fruit is the universe.
     There is nothing
     That cannot be determined by the word.

7.   It is the torch-bearer that illumines
     The path of right and wrong actions.
     It is the judge that hands down
     The decision between bondage or liberation.

8.   When it sides with ignorance,
     What is unreal appears real,
     And the real becomes valueless.

9.   The word causes the finite soul (jiva)
     To enter into pure Consciousness (Shiva).

10. The word liberates the finite soul
     Entangled in the body.
     The Self meets Himself by means of the word.

11. The Sun, by giving birth to the day,
     Becomes the enemy of night.
     It cannot, therefore, be compared
     To the word.

12. The word supports at the same time
    The path of action and the path of non-action --
    Even though they are opposites.

13. It makes of itself a sacrifice
    That the Self may be realized.
    How can I describe
    The many different merits of the word?

14. However, the word --
    So well-known as a reminder --
    Cannot coexist with the Self.

15. In the case of the Self,
    Which is self-luminous and without support,
    The word is absolutely useless.

16. There is nothing else beside the One Being.
    Therefore, it cannot be the object
    Of remembering or forgetting.

17. Can one remember or forget oneself?
    Can the tongue taste itself?

18. To one who is awake, there is no sleep.
    But is there awaking either?
    In the same way,
    There can be no remembering or forgetting
    To the One Being.

19. The Sun does not know the night.
    But can he know when it is day?
    In the same way,
    The One Being is without the ability
    To remember or to forget.

20. Then what is the use of a reminder
    Where there is no memory or forgetfulness?
    You see, the word is of no use
    In the case of the One.

21. There is another good result obtained
    Through the use of the word --
    But I'm afraid even to think about it.

22. It is foolish to say
    That the word destroys Ignorance, (1)
    And then the Self becomes conscious of Itself.

23. 'The Sun will first destroy the night,
    And then it will rise' --
    Such a false notion could never be stated
    Among intelligent people.

24. Where is that sleep
    Which an already awakened person can banish?
    Is there awakening
    In one who is already awake?

25. So, also, there is no ignorance to be destroyed.
    There is no such thing as a Self
    Desirous of becoming the Self.

26. Ignorance is as non-existent as the son
    Of a barren woman.
    Then what is there for the 'sword
    Of discrimination' to sever?

27. If the rainbow were as real as it seems,
    What archer would not have strung it?

28. I would vanquish ignorance
    By the power of logical thinking
    If it were possible for the water of a mirage
    To quench the thirst of Agastya.

29. If ignorance was something
    That could be destroyed by the word,
    Then could we not set fire
    To an imaginary city-in-the-sky?

30. Darkness cannot bear
    Contact with a lighted lamp --
    But was there really anything to be destroyed
    Before the lamp was lit?

31. Also, it is futile to light a lamp
    To illumine the light of day.

32. A shadow does not exist where it does not fall.
    Also, it does not exist where it does fall.

33. In the waking state,
    One knows that the dream one saw was false.
    Also, ignorance, though it appears to exist,
    Does not exist.

34. What could one gain
    By hoarding the wealth conjured by a magician?
    Or by stealing the clothes
    Of a naked beggar?

35. It is nothing more than fasting,
    Even though one might eat an imaginary sweet
    A hundred-thousand times.

36. There is no moisture in the soil
    Where there is no mirage.
    But is there moisture where there is one?

37. If ignorance were as real as it seems,
    Men would have been drenched
    By the rain painted in a picture;
    Fields would have been irrigated with it,
    And tanks would have been filled.

38. Why should one bother preparing ink
    If it were possible to write
    With a mixture of darkness?

39. Does not the sky appear blue to the eyes?
    The appearance of ignorance
    Is just as false.

40. Ignorance declares by its very name
    That it does not exist.

41. The fact that it cannot be defined
    Suggests its imaginary nature.
    Thus, ignorance proves its own non-existence.

42. If it really exists,
    Why can it not be determined by thought?
    If there is really a jar on the ground,
    It leaves a mark in the earth.

43. It is not correct understanding
    To say that the Self is revealed
    After the destruction of ignorance.
    It is like saying that the Sun is revealed
    After it destroys its awareness of darkness.

44. Ignorance, though illusory,
    Conceals its illusory nature.
    It proves its own absence.

45. Thus, as has been shown in various ways,
    Ignorance is by its very nature non-existent.
    Then whom should the word destroy?

46. If one strikes one's shadow,
    One strikes only the ground.
    Nothing is damaged by slapping empty space --
    Except one's own arm.

47. One may eagerly seek
    To drink the water of a mirage,
    Or to embrace the sky,
    Or to kiss one's own reflection --
    But all these efforts will be in vain.

48.   The logic that tries to destroy ignorance
      Is in the same category.

49.   If there is one who still has a desire
      To destroy this ignorance,
      He may, at his leisure,
      Peel the skin off the sky,

50.   Or milk the tits of a billy goat.
      Or see through his knees.
      Or dry out the night to make a tablet.

51.   Or squeeze the juice out of a yawn,
      And, mixing it with laziness,
      Pour it in the mouth
      Of a man without a head.

52.   He may reverse the flow of a stream,
      Turn over his shadow,
      Or make a rope of the wind.

53.   He may thrash an imaginary ogre,
      Tie up his reflection in a bag,
      Or merrily comb the hair on his palm.

54.   He may destroy
      A water-jar that doesn't exist,
      Pluck the flowers that grow in the sky,
      Or handily break the horns of a rabbit.

55.   He may prepare ink from camphor,
      Gather soot from the lamp-flame of a gem,
      Or happily get married to
      The daughter of a childless woman.

56.   He may feed Chakor birds
      With the nectar-rays of the waning moon,
      Or easily catch the water-fowl
      On the lake of a desert mirage.

57.   What more need I say?
      Ignorance is made of non-existence.
      Then what is there for the word to destroy?

58.   The word cannot prove itself
      By destroying what does not exist;
      Darkness cannot be made to comprehend
      The nature of darkness.

59.   Ignorance is never born.
      So what is the point of discussing its non-existence?
      It is like lighting a lamp
      In the courtyard at noon.

60. They who think to gather the harvest
    Before they have sown the seed
    Gather only shame.

61. One may as well
    Sit at home and do nothing
    As beg from a naked beggar.

62. Elucidation of the word
    Does nothing to destroy ignorance.
    It is like rain pouring on the ocean.

63. One may call oneself a measurer
    So long as one does not try to measure the sky.
    If light is able to perceive darkness,
    It is of no use.

64. If a tongue were able
    To taste a dish made from the sky,
    It would be meaningless
    To call it a tongue.

65. Will the gayly-colored garments
    Of a married woman
    Be appropriate at her husband's funeral?
    To eat the core of the plantain tree
    Is to eat nothing.

66. What object is there --
    Small or large --
    Which is not illumined by the Sun?
    But even he is of no use at night!

67. What is there that is not
    Perceived by the eyes?
    But they cannot perceive
    The sleep in a person who is awake!

68. Though the Chakora bird
    May look for the moon all the day,
    Its efforts are in vain.

69. One who reads a blank sheet of paper
    Remains as dumb as before.
    One who walks in the air
    Remains where he is.

70. In the same way,
    Words, attempting to destroy ignorance,
    Are but a meaningless jabbering.

71. On the day of the new moon,
    The moon sheds only darkness.
    Thought, attempting to destroy ignorance,
    Is in the same condition.

72. To make a meal of that food
     Which is not yet prepared
     Is the same as fasting.

73. In fact, the word
     Would accomplish its own destruction
     If it tried to explain the meaning
     Of something that does not exist.

74. Now, should I even say
     That ignorance doesn't exist?
     The word that tries to destroy it
     Vanishes itself.

75. If thought stands in front of ignorance,
     It destroys itself along with ignorance.

76. Ignorance, by its non-existence,
     Prevents the word from being
     Its vanquisher.

77. That the word should be so great
     As to become the revealer of the Self
     Is truly absurd.

78. Is there a country in which
     A person has married himself?
     Has there ever been
     An eclipse of the Sun by itself?

79. Can the sky be its own horizon?
     Can the ocean enter itself?
     Can a palm touch itself?

80. Does the Sun illumine himself?
     Does a fruit bear fruit?
     Does a fragrance smell itself?

81. We can easily enable all creatures to drink water.
     But, can we enable water to drink water?

82. Is there a day in the whole year
     Which the Sun is able to perceive?

83. If Shiva is angry,
     He may burn the three worlds.
     But will he burn fire also?

84. Is it possible even for the Creator
     To stand before Himself without a mirror?

85. It is certain that eyesight
     Cannot perceive itself,
     That taste cannot taste itself,
     That a person who is awake
     Cannot be awakened.

86. How can sandal paste wear itself?
    Or a color color itself?
    Or a pearl adorn itself with pearls?

87. Can gold be a touchstone to itself?
    Can a lamp give light to itself?
    Can a flavor enjoy its own sweetness?

88. Shiva holds the moon on his head --
    But can the moon wear the moon
    On its own head?

89. Likewise, the glorious Self
    Is, itself, pure and perfect knowledge.
    So how can knowledge know itself?

90. Being knowledge itself,
    He does not know how to know Himself.
    It is as hard as it would be
    For the eye to perceive itself.

91. Knowledge could know itself
    If a mirror could reflect itself
    In itself.

92. A knife may be able to pierce
    Anything in the four quarters --
    But can that knife pierce itself?

93. The tip of the tongue is very good
    For tasting different herbs and seasonings.
    But can it taste itself?

94. Does it therefore cease to be an organ of taste?
    No. It is because it tastes
    That it is an organ of taste.

95. So also, the Self,
    Who is Knowledge, Existence, and Bliss
    Is self-evident.
    How then can the word
    Offer Him what is already His own?

96. The ultimate Reality
    Does not prove or disprove Itself
    With the help of any other kind of knowledge.
    It is self-evident, Being in Itself,
    And beyond proof and disproof.

97. It is therefore groundless to believe
    That the word is so great
    As to be able to enable the Self
    To experience Himself.

98. A lamp that is lighted at midday
    Neither dispels darkness nor sheds light.
    It is the same with the word.

99. Since ignorance is non-existence,
    There can be no question of destroying it.
    And since the Self is self-evident,
    What is there to be proved at all?

100. Thus, being in both these ways useless,
     The word disappears --
     Like a stream in the waters
     Of the universal sea.

101. Right understanding shows that the word
     Cannot in any way approach the Self.

102. Just as it is meaningless to say
     That a dragon is coming,
     Or that the sky is clinging to your palm,

103. So also, the word, with all its associates,
     Becomes meaningless babbling --
     Like a picture with the colors all wrong.

*   *   *

Chapter Seven:

Refutation Of The Doctrine Of Ignorance

1. But for knowledge,
   Ignorance would never have shown itself.

2. A firefly appears as a light
   Only when it is in darkness.
   The idea of a beginningless ignorance
   Is utterly false.

3. The independent stature of ignorance
   Is like that of a dream,
   Or of darkness.

4. Horses made of mud cannot be harnessed;
   The jewelry conjured by a magician
   Cannot be worn.

5. This ignorance,
   Dragged from the house of knowledge,
   Can do nothing.
   Does a mirage appear in the moonlight?

6. What is called knowledge
   Is nothing but ignorance:
   Each appears at the concealment of the other.

7. Enough of this preamble --
   Let us begin our search for ignorance.
   Then, by understanding the true nature
   Of ignorance,
   We will understand the falsity of knowledge.

8. If there is really ignorance
   Within knowledge,
   Why does it not change knowledge
   Into ignorance?

9. For it is the inherent nature of ignorance
   To delude the one in whom it dwells.

10. If it is claimed by some
    That the sacred texts declare
    That the Self contains ignorance   (1)
    And is concealed by it,

11. I would answer:
    If the seed of ignorance dwells
    In that state where there is no rise of duality,
    Who, then, knows that it exists?

12. Ignorance, being nescient,
    Cannot know itself.
    Can it be a witness to its own existence?

13. No one could state that ignorance
    Is the cause of the knowledge of ignorance
    Without being aware of the contradiction,
    And would thus be compelled to silence.

14. If ignorance beclouds
    The understanding of the knower, the Self --
    Who, then, is there to call it ignorance?

15. And, if it does not conceal itself
    From Consciousness,
    Would it not be shameful to call it ignorance?

16. If the clouds really eclipsed the Sun,
    Who would illumine them?
    If a person were really annihilated by sleep,
    Who would experience it?

17. Therefore, if the one in whom ignorance resides
    Becomes ignorant,
    That ignorance cannot be discerned.

18. For that by which ignorance is discerned
    Can never be ignorance itself.

19. It would make no sense to say
    That there is a cataract in the eye
    But the eyesight is unimpaired.

20. If fuel does not burn
    When it is enveloped by a wild fire,
    It is useless as a fuel.

21. If there is darkness in a house
    But the house is not darkened,
    Then it cannot be called darkness.

22. Who would call that sleep
    Which does not disturb the waking state?
    Can that be called night
    Which does not cause the daylight
    To vanish?

23. The word 'ignorance' is meaningless
    If the Self is pervaded by it,
    And yet remains as it is.

24. Moreover, it would be logically incorrect
    To say that ignorance
    Resides in the Self.

25. Ignorance is the gathering of darkness,
    And the Self is the mine of effulgence.
    How then could they be mixed?

26. If waking and dreaming,
    Remembering and forgetting
    Could go hand in hand;

27. If cold and heat
    Could travel together to their place of rest,
    Or if the Sun's rays could be tied
    In a bundle by a rope of darkness;

28. Or if night and day
    Came to live together in one place,
    Then the Self might go on living
    By the aid of ignorance.

29. If death and life could be close relatives,
    The the Self might be dependent on ignorance.

30. How can it be said
    That the very ignorance
    That is dispelled by the Self
    Lives happily with it?

31. However, if the darkness gives up its darkness
    And turns into light,
    Then, of course, it becomes sunlight.

32. If fuel gives up its state
    And turns into fire,
    Then it becomes the fire.

33. Or if a small stream
    Gives up its separate existence
    By flowing into the Ganges,
    Then it becomes the Ganges.

34. In the same way,
    There is no ignorance.
    There is only the Self.
    As soon as ignorance
    Comes into contact with knowledge,
    It becomes knowledge.

35. Since ignorance is contrary to knowledge,
    It cannot retain its existence
    Within knowledge.
    Nor can it exist independently.

36. If a fish made of salt
    Becomes alive,
    It can neither live in the water
    Nor outside of the water.

37. Therefore, such statements as,
    'The Self shines where ignorance is absent'
    Should not be heeded by the wise.

38. A piece of rope
    Which is mistaken for a snake
    Cannot bind the imaginary snake,
    Nor can it be driven away.

39. Darkness, being frightened
    By the approaching daylight,
    Might turn for help to the full moon,
    But it would be immediately
    Swallowed up by that moon.

40. In the same way,
    The word, 'ignorance', is twice meaningless.
    The nature of ignorance cannot be understood
    Except by logical inference.

41. Then, what <u>is</u> its nature?
    Is it only <u>to</u> be inferred
    From the perceivable effects,
    Or can it be directly apprehended?
    Let us investigate.

42. Whatever may be apprehended
    By the various modes of proof,
    Like perception, and so forth,
    Is the effect of ignorance
    And not ignorance itself.

43. The creeping-vine has a beautiful sprout
    Which goes straight up;
    It is not a seed,
    But the effect of the seed.

44. One may see both pleasant
    And unpleasant forms in a dream;
    These are not sleep itself,
    But the effects of sleep.

45. Though the moon is one,
    It may be seen in the sky as two;
    This is not defective eyesight,
    But the effect of defective eyesight.

46. In the same way,
    The subject, the object,
    And the valid means of knowledge
    Are the effects of ignorance,
    And not the ignorance itself.

47. Therefore,
     The various modes of proof --
     Such as perception, and so forth --
     Being themselves the effects of ignorance,
     Certainly cannot apprehend ignorance.

48. If we regard the effects of ignorance
     As ignorance itself,
     Then even the senses of perception
     Must be included as ignorance.

49. If that which appears in a dream
     Is illusory,
     Then is the perceiver of the dream
     Also illusory?

50. If the effect of ignorance is also ignorance,
     It is like sugar tasting its own sweetness,
     Or collyrium putting on collyrium,
     Or like a stake being impaled on itself.

51. Likewise,
     If the effects are identical with the cause,
     Then all is ignorance,
     And who would know anything?

52. In such a state,
     One could not imagine a knower
     Or the known.
     It would be like taking the evidence
     Of a fish in a mirage.

53. So, my dear friend,
     What cannot be measured or defined
     By any proof whatsoever
     Is not different from a sky-flower.

54. Ignorance
     Does not allow of any proof of its existence.
     So how could one begin to discuss it?
     From this, one should understand
     The impossibility of ignorance.

55. Ignorance,
     Being neither an object of perception,
     Nor of inference,
     Is therefore disproved.

56. I am afraid to believe in this 'ignorance',
     Since it is neither the cause of anything,
     Nor the producer of any effect.

57. It can neither cause the Self to dream,
     Nor can it put Him to sleep
     In His place of repose.

58. Nonetheless,
    Some say ignorance exists in the pure Self,

59. As fire exists in wood
    Before two pieces of it are rubbed together.

60. But the pure Self
    Does not even admit the name 'Self'!
    How could ignorance expect to find room there?

61. Can a flame be snuffed out
    Before it is lit?
    Or can we leave the shade of a tree
    That has not yet sprouted?

62. Or smear salve on a body
    That is not yet born?
    Or cleanse a mirror that is not yet made?

63. Or skim the cream
    From milk that's still in the udder?

64. So likewise,
    How can there be ignorance in the Self
    Where there is not even room
    For calling it 'the Self'?

65. It should be clear
    That ignorance does not exist.
    And I wonder if it is even proper
    To give it the semblance of existence
    By stating that it does not exist.

66. If, in spite of this,
    One continues to say
    That ignorance exists in the Self
    Which is beyond all existence and non-existence,

67. It is like saying that an imaginary water-pot
    Has broken into a hundred pieces,
    Or that death itself had been utterly slain.

68. Or that unconsciousness had become unconscious,
    Or that darkness had fallen into a dark well;

69. Or that non-existence was in a quandary,
    Or that the core of a plantain tree was broken,
    Or that the sky, by turning into a whip,
    Was making a cracking sound;

70. Or that a dead man was being poisoned,
    Or that one who could not speak
    Was silenced,
    Or that unwritten letters were erased.

71. It is false to say
    That ignorance resides in the Self.
    That is tantamount to saying
    That they are identical.

72. But, can a barren woman have a child?
    Can burnt seeds sprout?
    Can darkness join the Sun?

73. No matter how we try
    To find ignorance in the Self,
    Which is pure Intelligence,
    It cannot be found.

74. One may stir up the milk to find the cream,
    But will it rise to the surface
    Or will it disappear?
    The search for ignorance is like this.

75. One may wake up quickly
    In order to catch hold of sleep,
    But will it be caught
    Or will it be inadvertently destroyed?

76. Therefore,
    Why should one madly search for ignorance?
    Such searching is equal to not searching at all.

77. The village of understanding
    Cannot be illumined in any way
    By the existence of ignorance.

78. Have the eyes of understanding
    Ever been able to see ignorance
    Either within or outside of the Self?

79. The face of discrimination
    Has never been washed by ignorance.
    Nor has ignorance ever admitted of proof
    Even in a dream.
    In fact,
    The thought that tries to grasp it,
    Loses itself.

80. Do you, in spite of all this,
    Think you will find some way to grasp ignorance?

81. You may as easily
    Build a town hall out of rabbit-horns,
    And light it with the rays of the new moon,

82. And celebrate
    By decorating the children of barren women
    With sky-flowers.

83. The desire to discover ignorance
     Will be fulfilled
     When we're able to fill the cup of the sky
     With the ghee made from a turtle's milk.

84. We have tried in so many ways
     To discover ignorance.
     How many more times must we repeat
     That it does not exist?

85. I would not utter the word 'ignorance'
     Even in a dream.
     But I have a thought about it
     Which I would like to share with you.

86. Suppose someone were to object in this fashion:
     "You say that the ultimate Reality
     Cannot see itself or any other object;

87. "Then how is it that It presents before Itself
     The entire visible universe
     And assumes the role of witness to it?

88. The entire universe rises
     And is visible to us,
     Who are in fact the Self.

89. "Though ignorance is not visible,
     Still it exists without any doubt.
     It is proved by inference
     From the visible world!

90. "The moon is one;
     If it appears in the sky as double,
     Would we not infer
     That our eyesight is impaired?

91. "The trees are fresh and green,
     And yet, it would appear
     That there is no water on the ground
     From which they grow.

92. "Therefore, we infer
     That their roots are absorbing water
     From below.
     Likewise, ignorance is inferred
     By the appearance of the visible world.

93. "Sleep vanishes as soon as one awakes,
     Nor is it known to the one who sleeps;
     Still, its existence may be inferred
     From the presence of dreams.

94. "So, if in the pure Self
    There appears this vast universe,
    We naturally infer
    The existence of ignorance."

95. To such an objection, I would reply:
    How can this kind of knowledge
    Be called 'ignorance'?

96. Can that be called 'collyrium'
    Which, when smeared on an object,
    Makes it whiter and brighter than the moon?

97. We may call this world
    'The unfoldment of ignorance'
    If water can behave as fire.

98. We may call that knowledge 'ignorance'
    If the full moon can be the cause
    Of a dark night.

99. Can poison release nectarean love?
    And if it does, can we call it poison?

100. Why should we bring in the tide of ignorance
     When all that is unfolding before us
     Is radiant with knowledge?

101. If we call this 'ignorance',
     What shall we call 'knowledge'?
     Is the Self a <u>thing</u>?

102. The Self does not become anything.
     He does not know what He is.
     All the means of knowledge vanish in Him.

103. He is not such as can be said to exist,
     Nor is there reason for saying He does not exist.

104. He exists without the existence of the 'other'.
     He sees without being the object
     Of anyone's vision.
     This being so, why should we regard Him
     As something to be found?

105. He silently endures
     The conviction of the Nihilists
     That He is nothing.
     Nor is He disturbed by those who regard Him
     As having particular attributes.

106. Do you think the omniscient One,
     Who is the witness of even the deepest sleep,
     Does not know about all of this?
     Still, He does not become visible.

107. The Vedas have said the same,
     Though they do not speak of 'the Self';
     They say only 'not this'.

108. Whom does the Sun not illumine?
     But does it illumine the Self?
     Can the Self be contained beneath the sky?

109. The ego considers only the body --
     Which is nothing but a bundle of bones --
     And says, "It is I".
     It takes no notice of the Self.

110. The intellect, which is able to grasp
     Everything that can be known,
     Falters before the Self.
     The mind can imagine anything --
     Except the Self.

111. The senses, that scrape their mouths
     On the barren land of sense-objects,
     Cannot taste the sweetness of the Self.

112. Is it possible
     To completely comprehend the Self
     Who has filled His belly
     With all that exists
     As well as all that does not exist?

113. Just as a tongue cannot taste itself,
     So the Self
     Cannot be an object of knowledge to Himself.
     How then could He be an object to others?

114. As soon as ignorance,
     With all her innumerable names and forms,
     Approaches the Self,
     It disappears out of fear.

115. How can anything else
     Find room in the Self?
     He does not even desire to
     See His own reflection.

116. There is a string-puzzle
     Which appears to ensnare a stick,
     But when the string is pulled,
     The onlooker is amazed
     To find that the stick is outside the puzzle.
     The effort to determine the nature of the Self
     Ends in this very same way.

117. One who minutely examines
     His own shadow,
     And then tries to jump over it,
     Has failed to understand its nature.

118. Also, the person who --
     After attempting to know the Self --
     Comes to this or that conclusion,
     Has failed to comprehend its nature.

119. Even words cannot reach
     To the place of the Self.
     How then can the intellect
     Comprehend Him as an object?

120. How can the absence of sight
     Be dispelled from the Self,
     And vision be imparted to It?

121. He cannot experience His own existence
     As an object of perception.
     Therefore, He cannot be a perceiver.

122. In such a case,
     Who will meet who?
     How can there be vision
     Where there is only One?

123. But He has flung open
     The doors of perception in man,
     And thus overcome this great obstacle!

124. Innumerable forms and visions arise,
     But it is one pure Consciousness
     Which is the substance of all.

125. The one underlying supreme Consciousness
     Is so intoxicated by the great glory
     Of this vision,
     That He does not see Himself
     In this mirror
     Wearing the same jewelry twice.

126. He has so much of riches
     That He causes Himself to appear
     In a novel array each moment.

127. He regards the objects of the world,
     Once created,
     As old and uninteresting,
     And therefore presents to His vision
     Ever-new and freshly-created objects.

128. As the perceiving subject,
     He is also incessantly changing
     The ornaments of His perception.

129. For, being bored with the solitude
     Of His original state,
     He has become many.

130. Such is the all-knowing One.
     As pure Consciousness,
     He is full to the brim.
     But that fullness is known
     Only in His own house.

131. That pure Consciousness,
     In whom knowledge and ignorance embrace,
     Meets Himself by having vision
     Of the many forms of visible objects.

132. Seeing the visible world,
     He enjoys it as its witness.
     That same bliss of enjoyment
     Pervades the entire array.

133. The interplay of give and take goes on,
     But the thread of unity is never broken.
     The unity of a person's face
     Is not altered by being reflected
     In a mirror;

134. Nor is the standing position
     Of a sleeping horse
     Disturbed when it awakes.

135. Just as water plays with itself
     By assuming the forms of waves,
     The Self, the ultimate Reality,
     Plays happily with Himself.

136. Fire weaves garlands of flames,
     But is it thereby ensnared in duality?

137. Is the Sun separate from the rays
     That radiate profusely from him?

138. Is the unity of the moon disturbed
     By its being enveloped in light?

139. Though a lotus-blossom contains
     A thousand petals,
     Still it is one.

140. In mythology,
     The king, Sahasrarjuna,
     Had a thousand hands.
     Did he then become
     A thousand different beings?

141. On a loom, many strands may be interwoven.
     But they are all only cotton.

142. Though a speech contains
     Ten thousand words,
     It is nothing but speech.

143. Though there are multitudes
Of visible objects,
And wave upon wave of images,
Still, they are not different
From their witness.

144. You may break a lump of raw sugar
Into a million pieces;
Still there is nothing but sugar.

145. Likewise, the Self,
Though He perceives images,
Or manifests Himself
In the forms of manifold objects,
Does not become thereby a different thing.

146. The unity of the Self is not lost
Even though He fills the whole universe.

147. Though a silk shirt
May be made of many colors,
With even a two-toned border,
After all, it contains only threads.

148. If the eye were able to see the whole
Without opening its lids,

149. Or if a banyan tree were to reach maturity
Without sprouting from its seed --
This would be comparable to
The expansion of the One into many.

150. When He strongly desires to see Himself no more,
He reposes within Himself.

151. It is comparable to the absorbing
Of vision into itself
When the eyelids are closed;

152. Or to the fullness of the ocean
Even before the hightide;
Or to the withdrawing of
A tortoise's legs into itself;

153. Or to the withdrawing of the moon's light
On the new moon day.

154. It is not that the Self is a conqueror,
As He is falsely called,
When He withdraws both the witness
And the visible objects.
It is simply that He is reposing in Himself.

155. There is no doubt that the Self
Is all that exists.
Therefore, who is perceiving what?
The state of non-perceiving
We can call His sleep.

156. If He says to Himself,
"I don't care for this state of non-perception;
I want to see Myself!",
Then He becomes an object to Himself.

157. The Self is the eternal perceiver
And the eternally perceived.
Now, what else needs to be created?

158. Does emptiness
Need to be associated with the sky?
Does the sense of touch
Need to be imparted to the air?
Does brightness
Need to be assigned to light?

159. The Self, shining as the universe,
Perceives the universe.
When there is no universe,
He perceives its non-existence.

160. And if, by chance,
The existence and non-existence
Of the universe
Were both perceived at once,
He alone is the perceiver
Of this state as well.

161. Does camphor derive its coolness
From the moonlight?
Is it not it own coolness?
Likewise, the Self is His own seer!

162. What more needs to be said?
Whatever condition the Self may be in,
He is seeing only His own Self --

163. Like one who discovers various countries
In his imagination,
And goes wandering through them all
With great enjoyment.

164. It is no wonder
That when the closed eyelids are pressed,
A pure brilliant light is seen
Vibrating there.

165. When it is always only
The one pure Consciousness seeing Itself,
Why postulate the necessity
Of a super-imposition? (2)

166. Does one cover a jewel with sparkle?
Does gold need to decorate itself
With shininess?

167. Does sandal wood need
     The addition of scent?
     Does nectar drink nectar?
     Does sugar eat sugar?

168. Does camphor need
     To be smeared with whiteness?
     Or does fire need to be heated
     In order to make it hot?

169. A creeping vine,
     Entwining about itself,
     Forms its own bower.

170. A lamp that is lit
     Does not need the addition of light;
     It is full of light.
     Likewise, the one pure Consciousness
     Is full of vibrant Radiance.

171. Therefore,
     Without obligation to anything else,
     He easily perceives Himself.

172. Perceiving and non-perceiving
     Are the same to Him.
     Is there any difference to the moon
     Between light and darkness?

173. Whether He desires one or the other,
     He is always of the same nature.

174. For a while, the Self appears
     As an object of perception.
     But when the seer and the seen unite,
     Both of them vanish.

175. Then the seen is the same as the seer,
     And the seer is merged in the seen.
     Both vanish,
     And only the Reality remains.

176. At any place and at any time,
     The seer and the seen
     May embrace each other, and merge.

177. Camphor does not become fire,
     Nor does fire become camphor.
     Both of them
     Are destroyed at the same time.

178. In mathematics,
     When one is subtracted from one,
     What's left is zero --
     And then that is erased.
     The same thing happens
     When the seer and the seen unite.

179. If someone attempts to wrestle
      With his own reflection in the water,
      Both the wrestling and the reflection
      Vanish together.

180. When the perceiver and the perceived
      Meet and unite,
      There is no more perception.

181. The eastern sea and the western sea
      Are different
      So long as they do not mingle.
      But once they have intermingled,
      There is only water.

182. Every moment new triads
      Of perceiver, perception and perceived
      Are emerging.
      Does each one need to be analyzed?

183. Every moment,
      A particular quality is swallowed up
      And its opposite emerges.
      This is the opening and closing
      Of the eye of Reality.

184. How amazing it is
      That when the eyelids are open,
      The Self becomes a perceiver
      Who vanishes when the eyelids are closed.

185. The natural state of the Self
      Lies between the destruction
      Of the perceiver and the perceived
      And a new revival of them.

186. It is like the natural state of water
      When the wave that has arisen subsides
      And a new one has not yet arisen.

187. Or like the state
      In which our sleep has ended,
      But we are not yet fully awake.

188. Or it may be imagined
      If we think of the sight
      Which has ceased to look at one object
      And has not yet begun to look at another.

189. It is like the state of the sky
      When day has ended,
      But night has not yet come;

190. Or like the state of the _prana_
      When one breath is finished
      And a new one is not yet taken in; (3)

191. Or like the state of a person
Whose senses are all enjoying their objects.

192. The ultimate nature of the Self
Is like that.
Then, can there be
Either seeing or non-seeing?

193. Can a mirror see its own clean surface?

194. By means of a mirror,
There is a face in front and a face behind.
But can that be so without a mirror?

195. The Sun sees everything.
But can he witness the beauty
Of his own rising and setting?

196. Can a juice drink itself?
Or does it hide itself from others
On that account?
It can do neither of these things;
It, itself, is juice.

197. He is vision itself;
He does not know seeing or non-seeing.
He, Himself, is the cause of both.

198. Being perception Himself,
How could He see Himself?
Of course, He is also non-perception.

199. How can non-perception perceive itself?
He is Himself perception!

200. These two -- perception and non-perception --
Dwell happily together
And are the destroyers of each other.

201. If seeing were able to see itself,
Wouldn't this be like not-seeing?
He is not touched
By either seeing or non-seeing.

202. If the Self,
Who can neither be seen or not seen,
Sees --
Then, who has seen what?

203. If the visible world appears,
Then has it not been perceived by the seer?
No. For it is not due to the appearance
That He sees.

204. The appearance is seen, to be sure;
     But the appearance is in fact
     Nothing but the seer.
     How can something else
     That does not exist be seen?

205. Supposing someone sees his own face in a mirror.
     That face actually exists in itself.
     But what is seen is unreal.

206. It is like seeing oneself in a dream,
     While asleep.

207. If someone dreams
     That he is carried away in a chariot
     To some other place,
     Is he really carried away?

208. Or if he dreams that a pair of headless beggars
     Have taken over the kingdom,
     Is it really so?

209. No. That person remains the same,
     Despite the dream,
     As he was prior to falling asleep.

210. The suffering of a thirsty person
     Is the same after he finds a mirage
     As it was before.
     What has he gained?

211. Or if a person strikes up an acquaintanceship
     With his own shadow --
     Of what use is that?

212. The Self as a witness,
     Has become the object of perception
     And then revealed it to Himself.
     But the revealing is really irrelevant.

213. Because, if what is seen
     Is nothing but the seer,
     How can the seer benefit by that revelation?
     Is He not present to Himself
     Even when He is not revealed?

214. Does a face become something less
     If it does not see itself in a mirror?
     It is what it is,
     Even without a mirror.

215. Likewise,
     The Self is not diminished
     If He is not revealed to Himself.
     Such revelation is really of no consequence.

216. The Self is as He is
Even without becoming a witness to Himself.
Now it may be protested:
"Why should He who is complete in Himself
Cause Himself to be an object of perception?

217. "It makes no sense to say
That what already exists is revealed;
Such revelation is pointless.

218. "It is the rope which actually exists,
Even though it appears as a snake.
It is the witness who really exists,
Even though he appears
As the object of perception.

219. "When a mirror is held before one's face,
That face appears obviously to be
In the mirror.
But, in fact, the face is
In its own place and not in the mirror.

220. "Of these two -- the seer and the seen --,
It is the seer who really exists.
What is seen, though perceivable,
Has no reality."

221. And I would answer:
Indeed, it has no independent reality.
But it does appear.
Does this not seem to prove
That it has existence?

222. If a person sees some other object,
Then we have a seer, the seen,
And the act of seeing.

223. But in the case of the Self,
He sees nothing other than Himself --
Whether He looks or not,
Whether He remains one or many.

224. A face sees only itself,
Even though a mirror has revealed it.
And that face remains the same,
In itself,
Even when it is not revealed by a mirror.

225. Likewise with the Self:
If He is revealed, He is as He is.
If He is not revealed, He is the same.

226. Whether a person is awake or asleep,
He is the same person.

227. A king, reminded of his kingship,
     Is certainly a king.

228. But is there any loss to his majesty
     Even if he is not reminded?

229. In the same way,
     The Self may be revealed or not revealed --
     He does not become greater or lesser.
     He always remains as He is.

230. Is there some other thing
     Which is eagerly trying to reveal
     The Self to Himself?
     But for the Self,
     Could there be a mirror?

231. Does a lit candle create
     The person who lights it,
     Or does it exist because of the person?
     Truly, the Self is the Cause
     Of all causes.

232. The flame lights the fire.
     But can it be regarded
     As something different from fire?

233. Whatever we call 'a cause'
     Is created and revealed by Him.
     By His own nature,
     He is whatever He sees.

234. The Self is self-illuminating.
     Therefore, there is no other cause
     For His seeing Himself
     Than Himself.

235. Whatever form appears,
     Appears because of Him.
     There is nothing else here but the Self.

236. It is the gold itself which shines
     In the form of a necklace or a coin --
     Because they are made of nothing but gold.

237. In the current of the river
     Or the waves of the sea,
     There is nothing but water.
     Similarly, in the universe,
     There is nothing which exists
     Or is brought into existence
     Other than the Self.

238. Though it may be smelled,
     Or touched, or seen,
     There is nothing else in camphor
     but camphor.

239. Likewise,
     No matter how He experiences Himself,
     The Self is all that is.

240. Whether appearing as the seen,
     Or perceiving as the seer,
     Nothing else exists besides the Self.

241. In the Ganges,
     Whether it flows as a river
     Or mingles with the ocean,
     We cannot see anything added --
     It is only water.

242. Whether it is liquid or frozen,
     Ghee does not become something else.
     It would be foolish to think that it did.

243. Flames and fire
     Are not seen as two separate things.
     Flame is the same as fire
     And is not different from it.

244. Therefore,
     Whether He is the seer or the seen,
     It doesn't matter;
     There is only the Self
     Vibrating everywhere.

245. From the standpoint of vibration,
     There is nothing but vibration.
     So, even though the Self sees,
     Does He really see?

246. It is not that the appearance is arrayed
     Here,
     And the seer is over
     There.
     It is only His own vibration
     That He perceives when He sees.

247. It is like ripples on water,
     Like gold on top of gold,
     Or eyesight gazing at vision.

248. It is like adding music to music,
     Or fragrance to fragrance,
     Or bliss to bliss;

249. Or like pouring sugar on sugar,
     Or covering a mountain of gold
     With gold,
     Or adding fire to the flames.

250. What more need I say?
     It is like the sky reposing on the sky.
     Who then is sleeping?
     And who is awake?

251. When He sees Himself,
     It is as though He did not see.
     And even without seeing Himself,
     He goes on seeing Himself.

252. Here, speech is prohibited.
     Knowledge is not allowed.
     Pride of experience can gain no entry.

253. His seeing of Himself
     Is like no one seeing nothing.

254. In short,
     The Self is self-illuminating.
     He awakens Himself without awaking.

255. Because of His desire to see Himself,
     He manifests all the various states of Being
     Without affecting His own state.

256. If He wishes to remain without seeing,
     Even that not-seeing
     Becomes seeing.
     And because of that seeing,
     Both seeing and non-seeing disappear.

257. Though He may expand into any form,
     His unity is never disturbed.
     And if He contracts,
     Then He is still as full as before.

258. The Sun can never catch up with darkness.
     Then why should he listen
     To talk about light?

259. Let there be darkness or light.
     The Self is like the Sun
     Who remains alone in his own glory
     Under every condition.

260. The Self may assume any form;
     He never strays from Himself.

261. Though innumerable waves rise
     And fall on the ocean,
     The ocean does not therefore become
     Something other than the ocean.

262. The glory of the Sun cannot be compared
To the glory of the Self,
Who is pure Light,
Because the Sun's rays go out from himself.

263. Cotton cannot be compared to Him,
For there would be no cloth
If the cotton pods did not burst.

264. Gold cannot be compared to Him,
For it cannot be made into ornaments
If it remains as it is.

265. No individual may be compared to Him,
For no one is able to go
From one country to another
Without crossing the intervening space.

266. So the play of the Self (Chidvilas)
Has no parallel.
He can be compared only to Himself.

267. He is incessantly devouring
Mouthfuls of His own light.
But neither is His store of light diminished
Nor is His belly expanded.

268. The Self,
Through His incomparable sport,
Is ruling His own kingdom
Within Himself.

269. If this can be called 'ignorance',
It means the end of all logical thinking.
Can we be patient with someone who thinks
This way?

270. If that which illumines is called 'ignorance',
It is like calling a miner's lamp
'a black stone'.

271. Would it make sense
To call a shining golden statue
Of the Goddess
'The dark one'?
Giving the name 'ignorance'
To the self-illuminating Self
Is like this.

272. In truth, all beings and all elements,
From Lord Shiva to the earth,
Are illumined by His rays.

273. It is because of Him
That knowledge knows,
Sight sees,
And light illumines.

274. Who, then, is that mean person
Who has designated Him as 'ignorance'?
Really!
Is it not like tying up the Sun
In a sack of darkness?

275. To write the letter 'A'
Before the word, 'jnana' (knowledge),
As a means of enhancing
The greatness of 'jnana'!
Is that not an extraordinary method
Of expanding a word's meaning?

276. What's the point of placing a fire
In a cardboard box?
It will only turn that into flames
As well!

277. It is pointless to speak
About the notion of ignorance
When the whole universe
Is the vibration of Knowledge.

278. First, it's like becoming guilty of murder
By uttering the word 'murder';
Secondly,
Such a notion is utterly false.
How, then, can Knowledge
Be called 'ignorance'?

279. Even to speak of ignorance
Is itself a vibration of Knowledge.
Then, mustn't we call knowledge
'Knowledge'?

280. By His own illumination,
The Self is perceiving Himself
In all these various forms.

281. How is it, then, that ignorance --
Which dissolves before the search light
Of thought --
Might acquire perception
And see itself as the visible world?

282. If ignorance states
That it gives birth to the world,
Which is Knowledge,
And attempts to establish its existence
By means of ignorance,

283. Then the world itself
     Has incontrovertibly proven
     The non-existence of ignorance;
     Because ignorance and Knowledge
     Are not things which can be related
     In the way that a substance
     And its quality are related.

284. Knowledge could be a quality of ignorance
     If pearls could be made with water,
     Or if a lamp could be kept lit with ashes.

285. Ignorance could emit the light of Knowledge
     If the moon could emit leaping flames,
     Or if the sky could be turned to stone.

286. It is certainly astounding
     That a deadly poison
     Could arise from an ocean of milk.
     But, can a deadly poison
     Give rise to pure nectar?

287. Even supposing
     That ignorance were produced from Knowledge,
     That ignorance would vanish at its very birth.
     Then, again, nothing would remain but Knowledge.

288. Just as the Sun is nothing but the Sun,
     The moon is nothing but the moon,
     And the flame of a lamp
     Is nothing but a flame --

289. Be assured also
     That the Light of Consciousness
     Is nothing but the Light.
     The whole universe
     Is nothing but the luminosity of the Self.

290. The scriptures declare with assurance
     That everything that exists
     Is radiating with His Light.
     Is it said for no reason?

291. The light of the Self
     Is Itself the cause
     Of the appearance of His beauty
     Which He Himself is enjoying.

292. To ignore this truth,
     And to regard ignorance as the cause
     Of the Self's appearance to Himself
     Is utterly unreasonable.

293.   Ignorance cannot be found to exist
       By any means.
       No matter how we may search for it,
       That search proves futile.

294.   Even if the Sun
       Were to visit the house of night,
       He would find no darkness.

295.   If a person attempts
       To catch sleep in a bag,
       He finds
       He cannot even catch wakefulness;
       He remains alone as he is.

*   *   *

Chapter Eight:

Refutation of Knowledge

1. As for ourselves,
    We possess neither knowledge nor ignorance.
    Our Guru has awakened us
    To our true Identity.

2. If we attempt to see our own state,
    That seeing itself becomes ashamed.
    What, then, should we do?

3. Fortunately,
    Our Guru has made us so vast
    That we cannot be contained
    Within ourselves.

4. We are not limited to being solely the Self.
    Nor are we disturbed
    By perceiving our limited existence.
    We remain always the same
    Even after final Liberation.

5. The word that can describe our state
    Has not yet been uttered.
    The eyes that can see us
    Do not exist.

6. Who, then, could perceive us,
    Or enjoy us as an object of enjoyment?
    We cannot even perceive ourselves!

7. It is no wonder that we can remain
    Neither concealed or manifest.
    Ah -- how difficult it is
    For us even to exist!

8. How can mere words
    Describe the state
    In which we are placed by Sri Nivritti?

9. And how can ignorance
    Dare to come before us?
    How can illusion
    Come into being after its death?

10. Can there be any talk about knowledge
    Where ignorance cannot gain entrance?

11. When night falls,
    We light the lamps.
    But what is the use of such efforts
    When the Sun is here?

12. Likewise,
    When there is no ignorance,
    Knowledge also disappears;
    Both of them vanish.

13. Actually,
    Knowledge and ignorance are destroyed
    In the process of discerning their meaning.

14. Both the husband
    And the wife lose their lives
    If they cut off each others' heads.

15. A lamp lit behind a person
    Is not really a light;
    If it's possible to see in the darkness,
    It's not really darkness.

16. Similarly,
    We call that which is utter nescience,
    'Ignorance'.
    But how can we call
    That by means of which everything is known
    By the name of 'ignorance'?

17. Thus, knowledge turns into ignorance,
    And ignorance is dispersed by knowledge.
    Each is cancelled by the other.

18. He who knows does not know,
    And he who does not know, knows.
    Where, then,
    Can knowledge and ignorance dwell?

19. Since the Sun of understanding
    Has arisen in the sky of pure Consciousness,
    It has swallowed up
    Both the day of knowledge
    And the night of ignorance.

*   *   *

Chapter Nine:

The Secret Of Natural Devotion

1. Just as fragrance might become a nose,
    Ears might emerge from a melody,
    Or a mirror might evolve from the eyes;

2. Just as fans might become a soft breeze,
    Heads might take the form
    Of Champaka blossoms,
    Giving forth a sweet scent;

3. Or the tongue might turn into sweetness,
    The lotus-bud might open as the Sun,
    Or the Chakor birds might become the moon;

4. Or flowers might take the form of a bee,
    A pretty girl might become a young lad,
    Or a person asleep might become his own bed;

5. As the blossoms of the mango tree
    Might become the cuckoo,
    One's body might become
    The Malayan breezes,
    Or flavors might become tongues;

6. Or as a slab of gold might become
    Pieces of jewelry
    For the sake of beauty,

7. Just so, the One becomes
    The enjoyer and the object of enjoyment,
    The seer and the object of vision,
    Without disturbing Its unity.

8. A Shevanti flower bursts forth
    With a thousand petals,
    Yet it does not become anything
    But a Shevanti flower.

9. Similarly, the auspicious drums
    Of ever-new experiences
    May be sounding,
    But in the city of stillness,
    Nothing is heard.

10. All of the senses may rush simultaneously
    Toward the multitude of sense objects,

11. But, just as in a mirror
    One's vision only meets one's vision,
    The rushing senses only meet themselves.

12. One may purchase a necklace,
    Earrings, or a bracelet --
    But it is only gold,
    Whichever one receives.

13. One may gather a handful of ripples --
    It is only water in the hand.

14. To the hand, camphor is touch;
    To the eye, it's a white object;
    To the nose it is fragrance,
    And nothing but fragrance.

15. Likewise, the sensible universe
    Is only the vibration of the Self.

16. The various senses attempt to catch
    Their objects in their hands --
    For example, the ears
    Try to catch the words --

17. But as soon as the senses
    Touch their objects,
    The objects disappear as objects.
    There's no object for one to touch --
    For all is the Self.

18. The juice of the sugarcane
    Is part of the sugarcane.
    The light of the full moon
    Belongs to the full moon.

19. The meeting of the senses and their objects
    Is like moonlight falling on the moon,
    Or water sprinkling on the sea.

20. One who has attained this wisdom
    May say whatever he likes --
    The silence of his contemplation
    Remains undisturbed.

21. His state of actionlessness
    Remains unaffected,
    Even though he performs countless actions.

22. Stretching out the arms of desire,
    One's eyesight embraces
    The objects she sees.
    But, in fact,
    Nothing at all is gained.

23. It is like the Sun
Stretching out the thousand arms
Of his rays
In order to grasp darkness.
He remains only One as before --

24. Just as a person arising
To enjoy the activity of a dream,
Finds himself alone.

25. Even one who has attained wisdom
May appear to become the enjoyer
Of the sense-objects before him,
But we do not know
What his enjoyment is like.

26. If the moon gathers moon-light,
What is gathered by who?
It is only a fruitless
And meaningless dream.

27. That yoga which yogis attain
Through restraining the senses
And other ascetic practices,
When placed before this path,
Is like the moon
Placed before daylight.

28. There is really no action or inaction;
Everything that is happening
Is experienced by the Self.

29. The undivided One
Enters the courtyard of duality
Of His own accord.
Unity only becomes strengthened
By the expansion of diversity.

30. Sweeter even than 'the bliss of Liberation'
Is the enjoyment of sense objects
To one who has attained wisdom.
In the house of Bhakti (devotion),
That lover and his God
Experience their sweet union.

31. Whether he walks in the streets
Or remains sitting quietly,
He is always in his own home.

32. He may perform actions,
But he has no goal to attain.
Do not imagine
That if he did nothing,
He would miss his goal.

33. He does not allow room
    For either memory or forgetfulness.
    For this reason,
    His behavior is not like that of others.

34. His 'rule of conduct' is his own sweet will.
    His meditation is whatever
    He happens to be doing.
    The glory of Liberation
    Serves as an asana (seat)
    To one is such a state.

35. God Himself is the devotee.
    The Goal is the path.
    The whole universe is one solitary Being.

36. It is He who becomes a god,
    And He who becomes a devotee.
    In Himself,
    He enjoys the kingdom of stillness.

37. The temple itself is merged
    In the all-pervasive God.
    The motion of time
    And the vastness of space
    Are no more.

38. Everything is contained
    In the Being of God.
    Where then is there room for the Goddess?
    Neither are there any attendants.

39. If a desire
    For the master-disciple relationship arises,
    It is God alone
    Who must supply both out of Himself.

40. Even the devotional practices,
    Such as japa (repetition of the Name),
    Faith and meditation,
    Are not different from God.

41. Therefore, God must worship God
    With God,
    In one way or another.

42. The temple, the idol, and the priests --
    All are carved out of the same stone mountain.
    Why, then, should there not be
    Devotional worship?

43. A tree spreads its foliage,
    And produces flowers and fruits,
    Even though it has no objective
    Outside of itself.

44. What does it matter if a dumb person
    Observes a vow of silence or not?
    Likewise, the wise
    Remain steadfast in their own divinity
    Whether they worship or not.

45. What's the point of worshipping with rice
    An idol of the Goddess
    That's made out of rice?

46. Will the flame of a lamp
    Remain without light
    If we do not ask her to wear
    The garment of light?

47. Is not the moon bathed in light
    Even though we do not ask her
    To wear the moonlight?

48. Fire is naturally hot.
    Why should we consider heating it?

49. A wise person is himself the Lord, Shiva.
    Therefore, even when he is not worshipping,
    He is worshipping.

50. Now the lamps of action and inaction
    Have both been snuffed out,
    And worshipping and not-worshipping
    Are sitting in the same seat
    And are eating from the same bowl.

51. In such a state,
    The sacred scriptures are to be censured,
    And censure itself
    Is like a sweet song of praise.

52. Both praise and censure
    Are, in fact, reduced to silence.
    Even though there is speech,
    It is silence.

53. No matter where he goes,
    That sage is making pilgrimage to Shiva.
    And if he attains to Shiva,
    That attainment is non-attainment.

54. How amazing
    That in such a state,
    Moving about on foot
    And remaining seated in one place
    Are the same!

55. No matter what his eyes fall upon
    At any time --
    He always enjoys the vision of Shiva.

56. If Shiva Himself appears before him,
    It is as if he has seen nothing.
    God and His devotee
    Are on the same level.

57. Of its own accord,
    A ball falls to the ground,
    And bounces up again,
    Enraptured in its own bliss.

58. If ever we could watch
    The play of a ball,
    We might be able to say something
    About the behavior of the sage.

59. The spontaneous, natural devotion
    Cannot be touched by the hand of action,
    Nor can knowledge penetrate it.

60. It goes on without end,
    In communion with itself.
    What bliss can be compared to this?

61. This natural devotion is a wonderful secret.
    It is the place in which meditation
    And knowledge are merged.

62. Hari and Hara (Vishnu and Shiva)
    Are, of course, really the same,
    But now even their names and forms
    Have become identical.

63. Oh, and Shiva and Shakti,
    Who were swallowing each other,
    Are now both swallowed up
    Simultaneously.

64. And even the subtlest speech,
    Eating up all objects
    And drinking up gross speech,
    Has now taken its rest in sleep.

65. O blissful and almighty Lord!
    You have made us the sole sovereign
    In the kingdom of perfect Bliss.

66. How wonderful
    That You have awakened the wakeful,
    Laid to rest those who were sleeping,
    And made us to realize
    Our own Self!

67. We are Yours entirely.
     Out of love,
     You include us as Your own,
     As is befitting Your greatness.

68. You do not receive anything from anyone,
     Nor do You give anything of Yourself
     To anyone else.
     We do not know how You enjoy Your greatness.

69. As the Guru, You are the Greatest of the great.
     But You are also very light --
     Capable of buoying up your disciples,
     Thus saving them from drowning in the world.
     Only by Your grace can these dual qualities
     Of Yours be understood.

70. Would the scriptures have extolled You,
     If Your unity were disturbed
     By sharing it with Your disciple?

71. O noble One!
     It is Your pleasure
     To become our nearest and dearest
     By taking away from us
     Our sense of difference from You.

                    *   *   *

Chapter Ten:

Blessings To The World

1.   O Sri Nivrittinath!
   You have blessed me
   With such sublime Bliss!
   Should I only enjoy it in myself?

2.   The great Lord has endowed the Sun
   With a fountain of light
   With which to illumine the entire world.

3.   Was the nectar of the moon's beams
   Given only for the moon's sake?
   Were the clouds given water by the sea
   For their own use?

4.   The lamp's light is meant
   For the entire household.
   The vastness of the sky
   Is for the sake of the whole world.

5.   Consider the surging tides
   Of the unfathomable sea;
   Are they not due to the power of the moon?
   And it is the spring season
   Which enables the trees to offer
   Their blossoms and their fruits.

6.   Also, it is no secret
   That all this is the gift
   Of your blissful divinity.
   I have nothing of my own.

7.   But why should I go on explaining like this?
   I only get in the way
   Of my master's glory!

8.   All that we have said
   Is already self-evident.
   Can words illumine the self-luminous?

9.   Even if we had kept silence,
   Would not someone have seen another?

10. When one person sees another,
    It becomes self-evident
    That the seer is also the seen.

11. There is no other secret
    About pure Understanding than this.
    And this is self-evident
    Before it is mentioned.

12. If it be said
    That there was then no need
    To begin to write such a work,
    I would have to reply that
    We are describing what is already self-evident
    Out of love for it.

13. It may be that we have tasted it before,
    But there is a new delight
    In tasting it again.
    To speak of what is self-evident
    Is therefore unobjectionable.

14. At least, I have not given out a secret.
    It is self-luminating.

15. We are immersed in the one perfect 'I'.
    We are pervading everything.
    Therefore, we can be neither concealed
    Nor revealed by anything.

16. What can we offer ourselves
    In the form of exposition?
    Would the Self be unexposed
    If we were to remain silent?

17. My speech is therefore the same
    As the deadest silence.

18. Even the ten Upanishads
    Cannot approach this silent speech.
    There, the intellect becomes
    Absorbed in itself.

19. Jnanadeva says,
    "This is the sweet Nectar of Self-Awareness.
    Even those who are liberated
    Should have a drink of it."

20. There is nothing wrong
    With the state of Liberation,
    But the Nectar of Self-Awareness
    Is so pure and sweet
    That even the timeless state of Liberation
    Yearns for a taste of it.

21. Every night there is a moon,
    But only when it gets the unobstructed
    Vision of the Sun
    Does it become full
    And shine its brightest.

22. A young girl possesses the bud of youth,
    But only when she is united with her beloved
    Does it blossom into flower.

23. Only when the spring season arrives
    Do the trees begin to kiss the sky
    With their branches
    Laden with fruit and flowers.

24. Likewise,
    I am now serving the dessert
    Of my spiritual attainment
    In the form of this
    Nectar of Self-Awareness.

25. Some souls have attained Liberation;
    Some are seeking Liberation,
    And some others are still in bondage.
    These differences remain
    Only so long as they have not tasted
    This Nectar of Self-Awareness.

26. Just as the streams
    Which come to play in the Ganges
    Become the Ganges,
    Or as darkness going to meet the Sun
    Becomes the light of the Sun;

27. Or as we may speak of different metals
    Only so long as they have not been touched
    By the philosopher's stone --
    When they all become gold --

28. So, those who enter deeply into these words
    Are like rivers which, mingling with the ocean,
    Become one.

29. Just as all possible sounds
    Meet in the sound OM,
    So there is nothing else --
    In all the world,
    But the Self.

30. It is impossible to point to anything
    That is not God.
    Truly, everything is Shiva.

31. Jnanadeva says,
    "May everyone in the universe
    Enjoy this feast
    Of the Nectar of Self-Awareness."

                    *   *   *

            Satgurunath Maharaj ki Jaya

HARIPATHA

Introduction To Haripatha

In addition to his main works, Jnaneshwari and Amritanubhav, Jnaneshwar composed several devotional songs as well. In them, he sings of his inner experiences and of his love for God and for his Guru, Nivrittinath. One such song is Haripatha, or 'Sing The Name of Hari', in which he utilizes a traditional poetic form to extol the practice of the repetition of the name of Hari, the name of God.

All the great saints of Maharashtra -- Nivrittinath, Jnaneshwar, Tukaram, Namadev, and Eknath -- wrote such Haripathas, declaring the chanting or repetition of the name of God to be the simplest, easiest, and surest way to God-realization. Jnanadev says,'chant within the name of Hari; your heart will melt with love. And that love will open the door to the true awareness -- that you and your beloved God are one'.

HARIPATHA

I

One who ascends, even for a moment,
To the threshold of God
Will assuredly attain the four stages of Liberation.
Therefore, chant the name of Hari --
Yes, chant the name of Hari!
The value of chanting His name is immeasurable;
So let your tongue eagerly chant Hari's name.

The authors of the Vedas and the various scriptures
Have all proclaimed this path with their arms upraised.
Jnanadev says: chant Hari's name;
The Lord will then become your slave,
Just as Krishna became the servant of the Pandavas --
As Vyasa, the poet, has so excellently told.

II

In all the four Vedas, Hari's praise is sung.
The six systems of philosophy, and the eighteen Puranas
Also sing Hari's praise.
Just as we churn curds for the purpose of getting butter,
Likewise, we churn the Vedas, philosophies, and the Puranas
For the purpose of tasting the sweet butter of Hari.
Hari is the goal; the rest is mere tales.

Hari is equally in everyone --
He's as much in all our souls as He is in the gods;
He's the inner Self of all.
Therefore, don't weary your mind with strange practices.
Jnanadev says: you will experience heaven
Just by chanting Hari's name.
Everywhere you look, you'll see only Him.

III

This insubstantial universe -- this web
Of interacting qualities --
Is but His superficial form.
His substance is the formless 'I'
Which is always the same,
Unaffected by the qualities' interplay.
If you discriminate in this way, you will understand
That continual remembrance of Hari
Is the supreme goal to be attained.
Hari is both the Formless and the changing forms.
Remember Him, lest your mind wander idly away.

He, Himself, has no form;
He cannot be seen.
He cannot be bound to a single form.
He's the Source of all forms,
Both the moving and unmoving.
Jnanadev says: Ramakrishna, the Lord,
Has pervaded my mind;
He is all I meditate on.
Blessed is this birth!
I seem to be reaping infinite fruits
From the good deeds I performed in the past.

IV

To speak of performing strenuous deeds
When all one's strength is spent
Is nothing but foolish talk.
To speak of one's love for God
When there's no feeling in the heart
Is also worthless and vain.
Only when true feeling arises
Can love for God bear fruit.
Will the Lord appear to you at your sudden call?
No. You must yearn for Him in your heart!

It's sad to see that you weary yourself
With so many worthless tasks.
Day after day, you anxiously fret
For your petty worldly affairs.
My dear, why do you never think
To turn to Hari with love?
Jnanadev says: it's enough
If only you chant His name;
At once your fetters will fall.

V

You may perform the rites of sacrifice,
Or follow the eight-fold path --
But neither will bring you to peace.
These are only tiresome activities of mind,
And usually bring only pride.
Without true, heart-felt love for God,
You'll not attain knowledge of Him.
How is it possible to experience union with Him
Without the Guru's grace?
Without the discipline of sadhana, He cannot be attained.   (1)

In order to receive, one must know how to give.
Give your love, and He'll shower you with grace.
Is there anyone who would be intimate with you
And teach you your highest good,
If you felt no love for him?
Jnanadev says: this is my judgement based on experience --
Living in the world is easy in the company of the saints.

VI

When one receives the grace of a saint,
His ego-consciousness dissolves.
Eventually, even God-consciousness will dissolve.
If you light a piece of camphor,
It produces a bright flame;
But after a while, both camphor and flame disappear.
In the same way, God-consciousness
Supplants ego-consciousness at first,
But eventually,
Even the awareness 'I am God' dissolves.

One who comes under the influence of a saint
Has arrived at the gates of Liberation;
He will attain all glory.
Jnanadev says: I delight in the company of the saints!
It is due to their grace that I see Hari everywhere --
In the forest, in the crowds, and also in my Self.

VII

Those who have no love in their hearts for God
Accumulate a mountain of sin
Which surrounds them like a diamond-hard shell.
He who has no love for God
Is totally deprived of love.
He who never even thinks of God
Is undoubtedly an unfortunate wretch.

How can those who are ceaselessly gossiping
Ever attain the vision of God?
Jnanadev says: That which lives
As the Self of everyone and everything
Is my only treasure.
That is Hari.
It is He alone I adore.

VIII

If our minds incline us to the company of the saints,
Then we'll acquire the knowledge of God.
Let your tongue be ever chanting His name;
Let your hunger be ever for Him.
Even Shiva, who is absorbed in his own Self,
Loves to hear the repetition of God's name.
Those who single-mindedly chant His name
Will realize Him, and be freed from duality.
They'll revel forever in the awareness of Unity.

Those lovers of God who drink the nectar of His name
Enjoy the same sweetness that yogis enjoy
When their Kundalini Shakti awakes.
Love for the Name arose early in Prahlada;
Udhava won discipleship to Krishna
Through his love of the Name.
Jnanadev says: the way of Hari's name is so easy --
Yet see how rare it is!
Few indeed are those who know
The infinite power of His name.

IX

He has no knowledge
Whose mind does not dwell on Hari,
And whose tongue speaks of everything but Hari.
He is a miserable person
Who takes birth as a human
And yet fails to seek the awareness of Unity.
How could that person find rest in the name of Hari?

Unless the Guru sweeps away the sense of duality,
How could he who has no knowledge
Relish the sweetness of chanting God's name?
Jnanadev says: repetition of the Lord's name
Is really a meditation on Him.
By chanting Hari's name,
All illusion is dissolved.

X

You may take a bath
In the confluence of the three holy rivers;
You may visit all the sacred pilgrimage places --
But if your mind does not always rest
In the name of the Lord,
All your efforts are in vain.
He is very foolish who turns away
From remembrance of God's name.
When the soul is drowning in misery,
Who else but God will rush to its aid?

Valmiki, who is certainly worthy of respect,
Has proclaimed the value of chanting God's name.
"The Name', he says, "is the one trustworthy means
For salvation in all the three worlds."
Jnanadev says: please chant Hari's name --
Even your children will be saved.

XI

It is enough to chant 'Hari' aloud;
In an instant all your sins will be burnt.
When a pile of grass is set ablaze,
The grass is transformed into fire.
Likewise, one who chants Hari's name
Becomes transformed into Him.

The power of chanting the name of Hari
Cannot be fathomed or gauged.
It has the power to drive away
All manner of devils and ghosts.
Jnanadev says: all-powerful is my Hari.
Even the Upanishads
Have failed to express His greatness.

XII

Taking baths in various holy rivers,
Observance of vows, and other such outward trappings,
Cannot grant fulfillment,
If in your heart no faith or love exists.
My dears, it seems that you're needlessly engaged
In the performance of unfruitful deeds!
It is only by the path of love
That God may be approached.
There is no other way.

Give love to God,
And He will be as tangible to you
As a fruit in the palm of your hand.
All other means of attaining God
Are like the attempt to pick up liquid mercury
That's been spilled out upon the ground.
Jnanadev says: I have been entrusted
By my Guru, Nivritti,
With the possession of the formless God.

XIII

Only when you have the continual experience of God
As equally existing in everyone and everything
Will you be truly established in samadhi.
This experience is unavailable to one
Who is addicted to duality.
Only when the mind
Becomes illumined by the experience of samadhi
Will it attain perfect understanding.
There is no higher attainment for the mind than this.

When one attains to God,
All miraculous powers are also attained.
But of what use are these powers by themselves
Without the bliss of samadhi?
In such a case, they are only obstacles
To one's progress on the path.
Jnanadev says: I have become supremely fulfilled
In the continual remembrance of Hari.

XIV

The Goddess of destruction will not even glance at you
If you chant fervently and unceasingly the name of Hari.
The chanting of His name
Is equal to a lifetime of austerities.
All your sins will fly away.

Even Shiva chants the mantra, 'Hari, Hari, Hari!'
Whoever chants it will attain Liberation.
Jnanadev says: I am always chanting
The name of the Lord.
That is how I have realized my Self,
The place of supreme inner peace.

XV

Let the chant of Hari's name
Be your sole determination.
Throw away even the mention of duality.
But, alas, such mastery
In the awareness of Unity is rare.
First you must practice the vision of equality --
Only Hari must be seen everywhere.
In order to do this,
The mind and senses must be restrained.

When all these essential requirements are attained,
One merges in Hari,
And becomes Hari, Himself.
Just as one solitary Sun
Manifests in countless rays of light,
One solitary supreme Being
Manifests Himself in all these countless forms.
Jnanadev says: my mind is fixed
On one unfailing practice --
The chant of Hari's name.
Thus, I've become free of all future rebirths.

XVI

It is an easy thing to chant the name of God,
Yet they are few who chant His name
With full awareness of its power.
Whoever has attained the experience of samadhi
By chanting His name
Has acquired all the miraculous powers as well.

If you unfailingly commit yourself
To chanting His name,
Then miraculous powers, intellectual brilliance,
And a disposition toward righteousness --
All will be yours.
Thus will you cross the ocean of illusion.
Jnanadev says: the Lord's name has become
Engraved upon my heart.
Because of this,
I see Hari, my Self, everywhere.

XVII

By chanting the name of Hari and singing His praise,
Even one's body becomes holy.
By practicing the austerity of chanting His name,
One makes a home for himself in heaven
That will endure for ages and ages.

By chanting His name,
Even one's parents, brothers, and other loved ones
Will become united with God.
Jnanadev says: the secret of His name's infinite power
Was laid in my hands by my Guru, Nivritti.

XVIII

One who reads the scriptures devotedly,
Who repeats Hari's name,
And keeps company with no one but Hari,
Attains heaven.
He earns the merit of bathing in all the holy rivers.
But piteous is he who chooses
To indulge his mind in its wandering ways.

He alone is blessed and fortunate
Who continues to chant the name of God.
Jnanadev says: I love to taste the name of Hari;
I meditate every moment on Him.

XIX

The proclamation and command of the Vedas
And all the holy scriptures
Is "Repeat the name of Hari --
The supreme Lord, who is the Source of all."
Without the remembrance of Hari,
All other practices -- such as rituals and austerities --
Are only futile exertions.
Those who have dedicated themselves
To remembrance of His name
Have found unending peace and contentment.

They have become enveloped in its sweetness
Like a bee who, in its search for honey,
Becomes enveloped in the closed petals of a flower.
Jnanadev says: Hari's name is my mantra.
It is also my formidable weapon.
Out of fear of this weapon,
The god of death keeps his distance
From me and from my family as well.

XX

The repetition of God's name
Is the only treasure desired by His lovers.
By its power, all their sins are destroyed.
The chanting of His name is equal
To lifetimes of performing austerities.
It's the easiest pathway to Liberation.

For one who chants the name of God,
Neither yoga nor yagna are needed;
The injunctions of 'duty' do not pertain to him.
He transcends all illusion.
Jnanadev says: no other ritual,
Or yagna, or rule of conduct is necessary
For one who chants the name of Hari with love.

XXI

There are no limitations of place or time
For the chanting of Hari's name.
Hari's name will save your family
On both your mother's and your father's side.
His name will wash away every blemish and stain.
Hari is the savior
Of all who have fallen into ignorance.

Who can think of a word adequate to describe
The good fortune of one whose tongue is restless
To chant the name of Hari --
The Source of all life?
Jnanadev says: my chant of Hari's name
Is always going on.
I feel that I have thereby made
An easy path to heaven for my ancestors as well.

XXII

There are very few who make the chanting of His name
An unfailing daily practice.
Yet, it is in this way that one may gain
The company of Hari, Lakshmi's Lord.
Chant 'Narayana Hari, Narayana Hari',
And all material happiness
As well as the four stages of Liberation
Will dance attendance at your door.

If there is no room in your life for Hari,
That life is truly a hell.
Whoever lives such a life will surely
Suffer hell after death as well.
Jnanadev says: when I asked my Guru
The value of the name of God,
Nivritti told me,
"It is greater than the sky above."

XXIII

Some philosophers say that
The universe is made of seven basic principles.
Others say the number is five,
Or three, or ten.
When Hari is realized, He reveals that --
No matter what the number --
All those principles emanate from Him alone.
But let us not be concerned with philosopher's games;
The name of God is not like that.
It's the easiest pathway to approach to the Lord;
It involves no strain or pain.

Some speak of 'ajapa-japa' (2)
As the practice that should be used.
This practice leads to a reversal of prana's flow.
To pursue this practice,
One needs much stamina and strength of will.
But the chant of God's name with love
Is free of all such difficulties.
Jnanadev says: I'm convinced that a man lives in vain
If he does not resort to the Name.
That's why I continue to extol
The chanting of the Name.

XXIV

The practice of japa, austerity, and rituals
Is futile without true purity of heart.
One must have the heart-felt conviction
That God lives in every form.
Please hold onto that conviction,
And throw away your doubts!
Chant aloud, 'Ramakrishna, Ramakrishna'
As loudly as you can.

Do not become conscious of your position and your wealth,
Your family lineage, or your virtuous acts.
All these considerations produce only pride.
Hasten only to sing Hari's name with great love.
Jnanadev says: Hari pervades my mind and my meditation.
I feel every moment that I'm living in Him.

XXV

To Hari, the learned and unlearned are the same.
By repeating His name,
Eternal Freedom is won.
The goddess of destruction will never even enter
That home where 'Narayana Hari' is sung.

How can we know His greatness
When even the Vedas could not explain Him?
Jnanadev says: this vast universe
Has turned into heaven for me.
Such luscious fruit has come into my hands
Only because I cling to His name.

XXVI

O my mind, cherish remembrance of Hari's name,
And Hari will shower His mercy on you.
It is no great difficult chore
To chant the name of the Lord.
Therefore, please chant His name
With a voice that is sweet with love.

There is nothing greater or more uplifting
Than the chanting of His name.
So why should you wander on difficult paths,
Forsaking the sweet path of His name?
Jnanadev says: I keep silence without,
And keep turning the japa-mala of His name within.
Thus, my japa is always going on.

XXVII

There is no pleasure as sweet as His name.
All the scriptures declare
That it's the secret to be attained.
So do not spend even a moment
Without enjoying the nectar of His name.
This world is only a superficial play.
It is only an imagination, after all.
Without the remembrance of Hari,
It's only a futile round of births and deaths.

By remembering His name,
All your sins will go up in flames.
Therefore, commit your mind to chanting Hari's name.
Take the attitude of adherence to truth,
And break the spell of illusion.
Do not allow the senses to bar your vision of the Self.
Have faith in the power of chanting His name.

Be kind, serene and compassionate toward all.
In this way,
You'll become the welcome guest of the Lord.
Jnanadev says: the chant of God's name
Is the means to samadhi.
This, I swear, is true.
This wisdom was bestowed upon me
By Nivrittinath, my Guru.

*   *   *

Satgurunath Maharaj ki Jaya

CHANGADEV PASASTHI

Introduction To Changadev Pasasthi

The story of Jnaneshwar and Changadev is a fascinating one. Changadev was also a great being. He had lived for a long time in heaven as a celestial servant of Indra. And then one day he was absentmindedly inattentive when an order was given, and Indra, in a fit of impatience, cursed him to live for a time as a mortal on earth. When Changadev prostrated himself before Indra and begged for mercy, Indra softened his sentence by saying, "You will be a suppliant to the incarnation of Vishnu, Brahma, Shiva and Shakti, who will appear on earth as Jnaneshwar, his brothers Sopan and Nivrittinath, and his sister Muktabai; you will attain God-consciousness, and then you will become a worshipper of Panduranga whose idol stands on the banks of the Bhima river. You will then live a family life and have children. You will enter samadhi without death. Then you will resume your former position in heaven."

Changadev then descended as a mortal into a lovely wooded spot on earth and lived there as a sage for some time. Though he had lost the memory of his former state, he still retained his celestial powers; and these supernatural powers soon became known to the nearby villagers. Thereafter, Changadev was venerated by thousands of disciples.

Not far away, in the town of Alandi, the boy Jnaneshwar was living, and Changadev, having heard tales of this amazing boy-saint, became curious about him and decided to meet with him -- thinking perhaps to show him up as an imposter. So he sent a letter to Jnaneshwar which, when Jnaneshwar opened it, turned out to be a blank piece of paper. Jnaneshwar, not at all intimidated by this, then sat down and wrote out a letter in reply to Changadev.

When Changadev received it and read it, he was awed and wonder-struck by the words of Jnaneshwar. How could a mere boy have written such a letter? Now he felt that he had to meet him. And so he set out with a huge assembly of devotees to Alandi, riding on a tiger and brandishing a cobra as a whip. It was then that the historic meeting of Jnaneshwar and Changadev took place. Jnaneshwar, spotting him riding toward Alandi, flew out to meet him, still perched atop the wall on which he'd been sitting, along with his brothers. And Changadev, realizing that he had met his master, reverently bowed in the dust before him. Thus he became a humble and loyal disciple of the great Jnaneshwar -- and lived to fulfill all the remaining prophecies of Indra as well.

The following is an English translation of the letter which Jnaneshwar wrote to Changadev. It contains in brief form the whole of Jnaneshwar's vision of Truth. It is full of compassion and love for Changadev, whom Jnaneshwar throughout the letter regards as equal and synonomous with the ultimate Reality, the Self. It is a rare and beautiful document, revealing the charming personality and flawless vision of a great being who has become fully and completely merged in and identified with the universal Self.

CHANGADEV PASASTHI

1. Salutations to the Lord of all, (1)
   Who is concealed within the visible universe.
   It is He who causes this universe to appear
   And it is He who causes it to vanish as well.

2. When He is revealed, the universe disappears;
   When He is concealed, the universe shines forth.
   Yet He doesn't hide Himself, nor does He reveal Himself;
   He is always present before us at every moment.

3. No matter how divers and varied the universe appears,
   He remains unmoved, unchanged.
   And this is just as one would expect,
   Since He is always One, without a second.

4. Though gold may be wrought into many ornaments,
   Its 'gold-ness' never changes.
   In the same way, He never changes,
   Though the universe contains so many varied forms.

5. The ripples on the surface of a pond
   Cannot conceal the water.
   This universe of many forms --
   Can it conceal His Being?

6. The element, earth, is not concealed
   By the immensity of the planet Earth.
   Likewise, He is not concealed
   By the immensity of the universe He inspires.

7. The moon above does not become hidden
   By the glory of its fullness,
   Nor does fire become hidden
   By its leaping, roaring flames.

8. It is not ignorance
   That causes the separation
   Between the perceiver and the perceived;
   Truly, everything is Himself, and He is the cause of everything.

9. Whether it is called a 'shirt' or a 'blouse',
   It is only the names that vary.
   It is clear that both
   Are only cotton cloth.
   Though different kinds of clay pots
   Are called by different names,
   Their varied colors cannot conceal
   The fact that all are made of clay.

10. The condition of separation
    Does not exist in one whose vision's clear;
    He remains alone, amidst all duality.
    To him, the perceiver and the perceived are one.

11. Though different kinds of ornaments have different names,
    All are made of gold.
    Though a body possesses several different limbs,
    Its unity is not disturbed.

12. It's the one pure Consciousness that becomes everything --
    From the gods above to the earth below.
    Objects may be seen as high or low,
    But the ocean of Consciousness, ever pure,
    Is all that ever is.

13. Though the shadows on the wall are ever changing,
    The wall itself remains steady and sure.
    Likewise, the forms of the universe take shape
    From Consciousness -- the eternal, primordial One.

14. Brown sugar remains brown sugar,
    Though it may be moulded into many forms.
    Likewise, the ocean of Consciousness is always the same,
    Though it becomes all the forms of the universe.

15. Various clothes of various patterns
    Are made from cotton cloth.
    Likewise, the varied forms of the universe
    Are creatively formed of Consciousness,
    Which remains forever pure.

16. Consciousness always remains in its pristine state,
    Unmoved by feelings of sorrow or of joy.
    Even though It may suddenly become aware of Itself,
    Its state and Its unity remain forever undisturbed.

17. The world that is perceived comes into being,
    And tantalizes the perceiver within --
    Though even the rays of the shining Sun
    Are but reflections of Its own eternity.

18. From within Its own divine pure depths,
    It gives birth to the perceivable world.
    The perceiver, the perceived, and the act of perception --
    These three form the eternal triad of manifestation.

19. In a spool of thread that's tightly wound,
    Nothing can be found of 'inside' or 'outside'.
    The thread is so intricately bound
    That its unity remains whole and undisturbed.
    Without the triad of 'perceiver, perceived,
    And the act of perception',
    One pure and primal Consciousness
    Enchantingly shines and sparkles alone.

20. Though It always has existence,
    It sees Itself only when this 'mirror' is present.
    Otherwise, there is no vision;
    There is only the awareness of Itself.

21. Without causing any blemish in Its unity,
    It expresses Itself through this triad as substance.
    These three are the ingredients
    In the creation of this perceptible universe.

22. When the 'perceived' becomes manifest,
    The 'perceiver' comes into existence simultaneously.
    And, by this apparently substantial world,
    The eyes become beguiled.

23. When the perceptible world is withdrawn,
    What can the eyes perceive?
    Can the eyes have any purpose
    If the objects of sight are not there?

24. It is only because of the existence of the 'perceived'
    That 'perception' can exist at all.
    If what is perceived is totally removed,
    What food shall the other two have?

25. Thus, the three dissolve into absolute unity:
    Then, only One remains.
    The three exist in the void of imagination;
    Only Oneness is real -- all else is a dream.

26. A face suffers no distortion
    Until a mirror is brought;
    Prior to that, its form and color are pure and true.
    What a difference when it's reflected in a mirror!

27. Thinking that It's there within the mirror,
    The Self reaches out to see Itself.
    The eyes become thoroughly beguiled
    When It confronts the image of Itself.

28. Before the world began,
    It remained in Its own state,
    Beyond 'perceiver' and 'perceived' --
    Aware only of Itself;

29. Like sound, where there is no bugle or drum;
    Or like fire, where there is no fuel to consume.
    Containing nothing in particular,
    It remained pure and clear, in Its original state.

30. It cannot be spoken of or spoken to;
    By no means may It be understood by the intellect.
    It is always existing full and whole,
    And so It shall always be.

31. The pupil of an eye
    Cannot see itself!
    True, it is the very instrument of vision --
    But it does not have such an ability as that.
    In the same way, even the Self-realized yogi
    Is helpless to see the Seer.
    Knowledge cannot know itself;
    The perceiver cannot perceive itself.

32. Where Knowledge is perfect and full,
    Ignorance cannot exist at all.
    So how could even the desire to know Itself
    Arise in Knowledge absolute?

33. Therefore, one should address It
    Through silence, by being nothing,
    If one would be free, all-knowing, all-pervading;
    For in that 'nothing' all power exists.

34. It is stated in all the holy scriptures:
    One Reality remains ever steadfast.
    Like water underneath the curling waves,
    That alone always remains.

35. It is Seeing -- without an object;
    It is Vision -- clear, perfect, and free.
    It exists alone, without anything else;
    Within Itself is everything -- and nothing.

36. Its existence rests on non-existence;
    It sees without any object to see.
    It enjoys without any object to enjoy;
    It is complete and whole in Itself.

37. Changadeva, you are a son of the Lord --
    As a piece of camphor is a son of camphor.
    O Changadeva, please listen to and heed
    These words I'm uttering to you.

38. Jnanadeva says to Changadeva:
    Your listening to my words·
    Is like my own hand
    Accepting the clasp of my other hand.

39. It is like words hearing themselves being uttered,
    Or like taste having a taste of itself,
    Or like a ray of light hoping to give light
    To other rays already bright.

40. It is like the attempt to improve gold
    By mixing it with gold,
    Or like a perfect face
    Becoming a mirror in order to see itself.

41. Our conversation, O Chakrapani,   (2)
     Shall be like that when we meet --
     Like the attempt to see one's own self
     By creating of oneself a mirror;
     Or like sweetness
     Trying avidly to taste itself.
     Would its mouth not overflow with itself?
     So also shall our mutual love.

42. O my friend, my heart expands with joy
     At the very thought of seeing you.
     But would it not be an error?
     Would not our already perfect union wane and die?

43. This desire of my mind to take such a form
     As you and I meeting face to face
     Arises suddenly in my heart with great warmth of love.
     But would it not debase our already perfect union?

44. And in your heart -- in your pristine, perfect state --
     The will to act, to speak, or suppose,
     Or not to act, to speak, or suppose,
     Does not even arise. So you see, it's a stalemate!

45. Changaya, in this pure name of yours,
     There is neither action nor non-action.
     What more can I say?
     Surely, there is no 'I'-ness in you at all.

46. A grain of salt went to fathom the ocean's depths --
     But when it became immersed, where did it go?
     What can it do and what can it measure
     When it has altogether ceased to exist?

47. My plight is like the plight of that grain of salt.
     Though I desire to see you, to play my role,
     How and where shall I find you?
     It is beyond my imagination to conceive!

48. Like one who awakes in order to encounter sleep,
     And misses encountering it,
     Here am I in order to encounter you
     Who are completely pure and free like Nothingness.

49. It is certain that there is no darkness
     In the light of the Sun,
     And it is just as certain
     That there is no awareness of 'I' in the absolute Self.

50. Thus, when I embrace you in purity,
     'I' and 'Thou' will swallow each other.
     Truly, our meeting shall take place
     When 'I' and 'Thou' are both devoured.

51. In the inner realm of vision,
    The eye is able to create all sorts of images.
    It is only in this way that it can see itself
    Without moving from its place.

52. Likewise, when words arise,
    Understanding tries to perceive their truth within.
    It is in this place of inner vision that we shall see
    The place where 'I' and 'Thou' both die.

53. Therefore, swallow altogether these limitations
    Of 'I' and 'Thou', and we shall meet.
    The pure harmony and joy of such a meeting
    We shall surely relish always.

54. It will be like taste eating itself
    For the sake of enjoying taste,
    Or like an eye becoming a mirror
    In order to see itself.

55. It is only by the 'words' of silence
    That nothingness becomes complete.
    It is with this garland of silent words
    That I went forth, and thus enjoyed the perfect meeting.

56. Please understand the meaning of my words,
    And thereby satisfy your hunger and your thirst.
    Regard yourself as a shining flame
    Burning brightly, without name or form.

57. These words are uttered simply
    To open the eyes of your inner Self.
    The perfect meeting with the infinite
    Is eternally within ourselves.

58. The rivers flow surely toward the sea,
    But when the final Deluge comes, both rivers and sea are submerged.
    In the same way, you should devour both 'I' and 'Thou',
    For truly, you are the Source of both.

59. Jnanadev says: you and I are One
    Without name or form;
    We are identical to the one blissful Existence
    In whom the blessed merge.

60. O Changaya, this knowledge has reached your door
    Unbidden, of its own accord.
    Go now beyond both knowledge and what is known --
    And reach the final state.

61. O Changadev! My Guru, Nivrittinath,
    Has spread this delicious feast for you
    With boundless, motherly love.
    Please enjoy its sweetness.

62. Thus, Jnanadev and Chakrapani
    Have met and merged,
    Like two mirrors reflecting each other
    In the eloquent silence that is Eternity.

63. If anyone were to read these verses,
    Using them as a mirror to see themselves,
    It's certain they would find
    The pure and blissful Self of all.

64. Where there is nothing, what can one know?
    The eyes can see -- but can they see themselves?
    How can knowledge be of use when all is oneself?
    To become one with the Self, surrender all the impulses of the mind.

65. Then you will know the 'sleep' beyond sleeping,
    The 'awake' which goes beyond waking.
    Now this garland is at last complete,
    Fashioned of the word-flowers which Jnanadev breathed.

                    *   *   *

            Satgurunath Maharaj ki Jaya

NOTES

Amritanubhav: Invocation

1.   <u>Nivrittinath</u>. Jnaneshwar here uses the name of his Guru as a synonym for God. It literally means 'Lord without <u>vrittis</u>', or mental modifications; i.e., the one in whom absolute stillness prevails.

2.   <u>Shiva and Shakti</u>. The one universal Reality which the sages realize through meditation is seen to have two aspects: When It is experienced as the whole, it is one; but it is also the multiple forms of the universe, and is therefore many. When it is experienced within as unity, it called Shiva; when it is experienced as the universe of multiplicity, it is called Shakti.

3.   <u>Shambhu</u>.   A name for God; literally, 'the Creator'.

Amritanubhav: Chapter One

1.   <u>Para to Vaikari</u>. In the philosophy of Shaivism, there are four levels of speech corresponding to the four bodies of man, each subtler than the one before. <u>Vaikari</u>, the gross speech, emanates from <u>madhyama</u>, the subtle speech -- which emanates from <u>pashyanti</u>, the causal level -- which emanates from <u>para</u>, the supra-causal level. <u>Para</u>, the place where the initial thought-impulse originates, emanates from the perfect silence of the Absolute, the Self.

2.   <u>Plantain tree</u>. The plantain tree, said to be hollow at its core, serves as a common metaphorical image to convey the idea of the identity of the inner and outer, the individual soul and the universal Soul.

Amritanubhav: Chapter Two

1.   <u>Guru</u>. By the power of his own awareness of the Self, the Guru, simply by a glance, can awaken the disciple. He acts as a clear channel for the grace of God, and the disciple's worthiness draws that grace from him. With one compassionate look, or even by his mere will, he enables the disciple to pierce the veil of Maya, and realize his own Being.

Amritanubhav: Chapter Six

1.   <u>Ignorance</u>. By ignorance (<u>avidya</u>, or <u>ajnana</u>), is meant the primary veil of unknowing which conceals from the individual Self Its own true nature. Jnaneshwar argues that this 'ignorance' is a phantom, existing only so long as one gives it existence by not-knowing. It ceases to exist simultaneous with the arising of knowledge, just as darkness ceases to exist simultaneous with the Sun's rising, without the need for any secondary means or act to dispel it.

Amritanubhav: Chapter Seven

1.   Claimed by some. Jnaneshwar is here referring to the
Vedantic scholars of his own time who stated that ignorance, as a
sort of veiling power, resides in a seed-form within the absolute
Consciousness, the universal Self. In fact, as Jnaneshwar points
out, ignorance is not a thing; nor is it a cause -- it has no
causal power. It is an effect -- an effect of the Self's will
to manifest in form. When one is immersed in consciousness of
the Self, there can be no ignorance. Ignorance only makes its
appearance when consciousness gives birth to duality in the form
of knowledge and ignorance. For one who has once become established
in the consciousness of the Self, this birth does not take place.
And therefore ignorance is seen as a non-entity.

2.   Super-imposition. Again, Jnaneshwar is addressing the
Vedantic philosophers, who uphold the view that the world is a
'super-imposition' on Brahman, the Absolute, just as a snake might
be super-imposed on a rope seen lying on a road. Jnaneshwar shows
up the confusion inherent in this line of thinking. It is not
that the Self is being overlaid by an imaginary image, or that
something is being seen in it that is not there; It is one thing.
It appears as It does simply because that's the way the Self appears
to the eyes.

3.   Prana. Jnaneshwar is here describing a technique for attain-
ing the realization of the Self. It is said in the Shaivite scriptures
that God dwells in the space between the breaths. As the breath comes
in, it makes the sound Ham; as it goes out, it makes the sound Sah.
In the juncture where Ham gives rise to Sah, and in the juncture
where Sah gives rise to Ham, one may realize the stillness from which
all sounds arise. In this state of equalibrium, the Self reveals
Itself.

Haripatha: Chapter Five

1.   Sadhana. Sadhana here means not only 'spiritual endeavor',
but that endeavor done under the supervision of a true Guru, who is
capable of awarding grace.

Haripatha: Chapter Twenty-three

2.   Ajapa-japa. Ajapa japa is that repetition of God's name
which requires no repetition; it is in fact a listening to the breath
as it comes in and goes out, with the awareness of Ham Sah, 'I am That'.

Changadev Pasasthi: Chapter One

1.   Lord of all. In the original Marathi language, Jnaneshwar
addresses Changadev as Sri Vateshwar, which is both a nickname of
Changadev and a name for God. He thereby raises Changadev immediately
to the status of the pure Self of all, thus uprooting his identification
with the limited form.

2.   <u>Chakrapani</u>. Chakrapani is a name for Krishna, the manifestation of the Godhead. Here again, Jnaneshwar is equating Changadev with the highest, the Soul of all, and stealing away his sense of separation from that universal Soul.

*   *   *

other publications

By Swami Muktananda

Play of Consciousness Muktananda's spiritual autobiography
Satsang With Baba (Five Volumes) Questions and answers
Getting Rid of What You Haven't Got* Informal interviews and talks
Muktananda-Selected Essays Edited by Paul Zweig
Light on the Path Essential aspects of the Siddha Path
Siddha Meditation* Commentaries on the Shiva Sutras and other ancient scriptures
Mukteshwari I & II Poetic aphorisms
In the Company of a Siddha Baba talks with pioneers in science, consciousness and
    spirituality
I Am That The science of Hamsa mantra
Kundalini The Secret of Life
I Welcome You All With Love "Little book" of aphorisms
God Is With You "Little book" of aphorisms
Sadgurunath Maharaj Ki Jaya Photos and essays of the 1974 Australian tour
Ashram Dharma Guidance for Ashram living
A Book for the Mind Aphorisms on the mind
I Love You* Aphorisms on love
What is an Intensive? Muktananda's 2-day program for spiritual awakening
Bhagawan Nityananda Portrait of Baba's Guru, Swami Nityananda
So'ham Japa Spontaneous inner mantra repetition
Swami Muktananda in Australia Talks given during the 1970 tour
Swami Muktananda American Tour 1970 Talks from Baba's first visit to the U.S.

About Swami Muktananda

Swami Muktananda Paramahansa* by Amma (Swami Prajnananda) Muktananda
    biography
Sadhana Photographic essay of Muktananda's spiritual practice
Muktananda Siddha Guru* by Shankar (Swami Shankarananda) Very clear intro-
    duction to Baba and his teachings
Japan Hijack by Narayan Krueger A devotee's international adventure

Other Books

Introduction to Kashmir Shaivism The philosophy most closely reflecting Baba's
    teaching
Siddha Cooking Secrets of Baba's delicious food
Nectar of Chanting Sacred chants sung regularly in Baba's Ashrams; Sanskrit trans-
    lation with transliteration

Publications

Muktananda The Siddha Path Monthly magazine of S.Y.D.A. Foundation
Gurudev Siddha Peeth Newsletter Monthly from Baba's Ashram in India
Shree Gurudev Vani Annual Journal by devotees

*Also available in Braille Complete with photographs

If you want more information about these books, write to
SYDA Bookstore, P.O. Box 605, South Fallsburg, N.Y. 12779

directory

There are more than 250 Siddha Yoga Meditation Centers and residential Ashrams around the world. To find out if there is a Center near you, you may contact the SYDA Centers Office, 324 W. 86 St., N.Y.C., (212) 874-8030.

UNITED STATES

SYDA Foundation   P.O. Box 605, South Fallsburg, N.Y. 12779

Siddha Yoga Dham Ann Arbor   1520 Hill, Ann Arbor, Michigan 48104, Phone: (313) 994-5625

Siddha Yoga Dham Boston   Fernwood Road/Manor House, Brookline, Massachusetts 02167, Phone: (617) 734-0137

Siddha Yoga Meditation Ashram Chicago   2100 W. Bradley Place, Chicago, Illinois 60618, Phone: (312) 327-0536

Siddha Yoga Dham Hawaii   P.O. Box 10191, Honolulu, Hawaii 96816, 3807 Diamond Head Circle, Honolulu, Hawaii 96815, Phone: (808) 732-1558

Siddha Yoga Dham Houston   3815 Garrett, Houston, Texas 77006, Phone: (713) 529-0006

Siddha Yoga Dham Los Angeles   605 S. Mariposa, Los Angeles, California 90005, Phone: (213) 386-2328

Siddha Yoga Dham Manhattan   324 West 86th Street, New York, New York 10024, Phone: (212) 873-8030

Siddha Yoga Dham Miami   c/o Arunski, 8264 SW 184th Terrace, Miami, Florida 33157

Siddha Yoga Dham Oakland   1107 Stanford Avenue, Oakland, California 94608, P.O. Box 11071, Oakland, California 94611, Phone: (415) 655-8677

Siddha Yoga Dham Philadelphia   6429 Wayne Avenue, Philadelphia, Pennsylvania 19119, Phone: (215) 849-0888

Siddha Yoga Dham Seattle   c/o Ihli, 15709 25th S.W., Seattle, Washington 98102, Phone: (206) 325-2642

Muktananda Siddha Meditation Center Washington D.C.   c/o Mundra, 2900 Conn. Ave. N.W. 26, Washington D.C. 20008, Phone: (202) 483-4849

AUSTRALIA

Siddha Yoga Dham Melbourne   202 Gore Street, Fitzroy, Melbourne VIC 3065 Australia, Phone: (03)419-6299

CANADA

Siddha Yoga Dham Canada   c/o Padmanabhan, 10051 4th Avenue, Richmond BC V7E 1V4 Canada, Phone: (604) 274-9008

ENGLAND

Siddha Yoga Dham London   1 Bonneville Gardens, London SW4 England Phone: (01)675-4105

FRANCE

Siddha Yoga Dham France　　c/o de Pardieu, 8 rue Freycinet, 75116 Paris, France, Phone: 720-8430

GERMANY

Siddha Yoga Dham Germany　　c/o Resnizek, Fischergasse 5, 6050 Offenbach, West Germany, Phone: 0611-86-12-60

INDIA

Gurudev Siddha Peeth　　P.O. Ganeshpuri (Pin 401 206), Dist. Thana, Maharashtra, India

Shree Gurudev Ashram　　Village Bhatti, Mehruli, New Delhi South, India 110 030

ISRAEL

Siddha Yoga Dham Jerusalem　　c/o Bar-Yehudad, P.O. Box 11001 Jerusalem Israel

MEXICO

Siddha Yoga Dham Mexico City　　c/o Fernandez, Apartado 41-890, Mexico 10 DF Mexico, Phone: (905) 545-9375

NETHERLANDS

Muktananda Siddha Meditation Center Amsterdam　　c/o Haberland and Heery, Laing's Nekstraat 66hs, 1092 GZ Amsterdam, Netherlands, Phone: 020-23.29.92

SOUTH AFRICA

Shree Gurudev Dhyan Mandir　　c/o Patel, 42a Clare Rd., Fordsburg 2033, Johannesburg, South Africa

SPAIN

Centro de Meditacion Muktananda Barcelona　　Gran Via, 434 #3, Barcelona 15, Spain Phone: (93) 235-2197

SWITZERLAND

Muktananda Siddha Meditation Center Bern　　c/o Carter, Brunngasse 54, 3011, Bern, Switzerland   Phone: (031) 22.59.63

SWEDEN

Siddha Yoga Dham Stockholm　　c/o Gustavsson-Nameth, Kapellgrand 17A, S-116 21 Stockholm, Sweden, Phone: (08) 43-57-09